I HEARD A CROW CALL MY NAME

I HEARD A CROW CALL MY NAME

Rodney R. Romney

This is an account of a true life experience by the author, embellished at certain times into the realm of fantasy.

This book was printed in the United States of America.

To order additional copies of this book, contact:
Xlibris Corporation
1-888-795-4274
www.Xlibris.com
Orders@Xlibris.com
35986

CONTENTS

Preface

The title of this memoir is not meant to be disrespectful of Margaret Craven's beautiful and heartwarming novel, *I Heard the Owl Call My Name* (Doubleday, 1973). Hers is the story of a young priest's discovery of the ultimate truths of life and death while living among the Indians of the Northwest, who believed that when it was your time to die, you would be given precognition by hearing an owl call your name.

I Heard a Crow Call My Name, or if you prefer, *I Heard a Crow Caw My Name*, is a story about my coming to a deeper and fuller appreciation of life by discovering the wonderful world of communication that can exist between humans and animals.

There is much in our world to cause concern. Conflict, misery, and distrust often prevent us from experiencing the deepest essentials of life. I would like to believe that through a simple and comparatively uncomplicated relationship with a crow, which lived in the trees above my yard, I gained a new perspective on the lasting values of compassion, unselfishness, honesty, humility, and fun.

The Bible tells us there was once a time when the earth was of one language and speech, and all things were in unity and accord. Humans and nonhumans shared a common language and were able to communicate freely and openly with one another. Was this story just a myth, the result of someone's wistful thinking? Or is it possible that accord and correspondence between humans and animals are part of the Great Cosmic Plan? If so, then perhaps there is a universal language that we have somehow forgotten how to speak, one that will bring us into the gracious unfoldment of the Plan. That is a little of what this book is about. It is also about a crow I named Charlie who has carefully watched over its writing in a manner that revealed he has an even bigger stake than I have in the story.

Chapter One

I Heard a Crow Call My Name

One beautiful spring morning, I was walking up the road that leads from our house on the Puget Sound to the hill above, as I do with some regularity. The air was fragrant with the scent of recent rains, wakened trees, and freshly polished stones. I came upon a crow in the middle of the road, pecking furiously at something wrapped in a cellophane ziplock bag. As I got closer, the crow emitted a disgusted squawk and flew to an overhead tree. There in the street lay a package of pita bread, either discarded by someone in a garbage pail because it had gotten stale or filched by the crow from a grocery bag that had been left unattended on a porch. The crow's beak had dented but not succeeded in breaking through the tough cellophane. I picked it up. The crow cawed an order to me, "Open it!" There was no mistaking its meaning. I opened the bag, took out the bread, spread it in the street, and walked on. As I glanced back, four crows were in the road busily stockpiling the bread in their beaks, after which they flew off.

I continued to the top of the hill, where I stopped at an espresso stand and bought a hot drink and a bun to munch on my way back home. Striding down the hill, I came to the spot where I had assisted the crow in his theft of the pita bread. There he was, perched in the same tree, awaiting my approach. As I came near, chomping on the bun, he squawked another order. "Share it." I broke off a piece and dropped it in the road. Immediately he swooped down and picked it up in his beak. For the rest of my walk, until I reached home, the crow stalked me from the air, calling out his order to share with him what I had. By the time I completed my walk, Mr. Crow had managed to get the larger share of the bun. He flew to a tree above our house; and as I prepared to go in, he saluted me with a noisy, "Later, dude." It carried a hint of more to come.

That was the beginning of my relationship with the crow I decided to name Charlie. The next morning, as I sat at the kitchen bar eating breakfast, he called to me from a leafy perch outside the window. I had the eerie feeling he could see through the walls and knew exactly where I was and what I was doing. I carried a piece of toast outside, broke it into pieces, and dropped it on the ground. At once Charlie flew down to pick up as many pieces as he could and then soared toward the top of a fir near our house. In just such a simple, unsuspecting way, I allowed him to establish the ritual that was to continue. Each morning he would sit in the maple tree outside my window and watch me eat breakfast. When I was finished, he would remind me with his raucous one-note message that I had not yet shared anything with him.

Later he would introduce me to his mate, Clarabelle, and even later, to his children, Clancy and Crista. I gave them all *C* names; possibly I was in love with alliteration at the time. They were followed by his sisters, brothers, cousins, aunts and uncles, and God only knows who else. For the past five years or so, Charlie and his expanded family have been my "fine feathered friends" and my daily companions.

How can I tell Charlie apart from others? Visually I cannot. Except for size and an occasional battle mark or blemish, all crows look alike. The difference is in their behavior. Charlie was the one who was never afraid of me, who would not wait until I went into the house before plummeting down to eat whatever food I strewed on the ground. Charlie was the one who made passes over my head as I walked, calling to me with a playful cluck. I knew him not by his appearance but by his behavior.

Though our ritual began with food, it quickly became more than that. Only if you have experienced it can you know the wonderful feeling of having a bird sweep down out of the sky to sit beside you. There is no greater sense of knowing than that which develops between a human and an animal, especially a wild one, for it depends on something deeper than words. There is no greater pleasure than watching a bird turn spirals over your head, side and back flips, before swooping down in front of you, and to know it is all because of his pleasure at seeing you. It didn't all happen at once, but little by little, we became friends. Call me an old romantic fool if you wish. I only know that one spring morning I heard a crow call my name and have never been quite the same since that time.

I have decided to let Charlie be part of the voice that tells this story. Before he does that, I want to share a bit of what I have learned about crows since I met him. I had always thought of them as noisy, aggressive birds that are nest predators and scavengers of garbage. They don't have a sweet call; indeed their song is more an assault than a serenade. They are big, and worse, they are black. Very black. Black is the color that symbolizes death; so in ancient legends and myths, crows have been unfairly labeled as witches, devils, and representatives of doom. It was the raven, remember, who quoted the fatal "Nevermore" to poet Edgar Allan Poe's yearning for happiness.

Only recently have we humans begun to show more interest in crows and have discovered something of their unique behaviors and innate intelligence. They are not only smart and savvy, they are also brave and funny. Tony Angell, Seattle educator and author of *Ravens, Crows, Magpies, and Jays*, labeled them "airborne Einsteins," and more than one writer has sung the praises of the crow as "something to crow about."

Scientists have now proved that crows have relatively large brains. In fact, they are so smart that it is difficult to catch them and mark them individually. Rev. Henry Ward Beecher in the mid-1800s said, "If men had wings and bore black feathers, few of them would be clever enough to be crows."

I am indebted to several writers for their research, who have helped me understand these remarkable birds, especially Candace Savage (*Bird Brains: The Intelligence of Crows, Ravens, Magpies, and Jays*, Sierra Club Books, 1995) and Bernd Heinrich (*Ravens in Winter*, Vintage, 1991). Their work is fascinating and truly monumental in showing how adaptable, inventive, and lovable these birds often are.

Ravens and crows come from the same family, although crows are smaller than ravens, inhabit different geographic regions, and have distinctive characteristics. There is a saying, "If it hops, it's a raven; if it walks, it's a crow." In the Pacific Northwest where I live, we do not have ravens; we have what some call Northwest crows. Jays and magpies come from the same family, Corvidae. Bernd Heinrich breaks that family down into different groupings and details their distinctions for those who want to know more.

Crows are all scavengers and will eat animal flesh, insects, vegetables, and grains—with a particular preference for corn. Despite what I've heard people say, crows do not like everything. Charlie once spit out a piece of stale broccoli, which was coated in a weathered cheese sauce, making a noise that sounded like *phewy*; and with such force, it sailed clear across the lawn. I don't know if Charlie didn't like stale food that day, or if, like me, he didn't care for broccoli.

Crows build durable nests of sticks lined with grass, moss, and anything soft they can find. Usually these nests are located in tall trees; although in urban areas, crows have been known to nest on the tops of telephone poles. It is believed crows mate for life. They will lay four to six eggs a year, but in urban areas, usually no more than two of the nestlings survive. The young will stay close to the nest, following their parents about for several weeks, noisily demanding to be fed while learning how to find their own food. When the young are able to fend for themselves, the family will join other groups of crows, where they will feed and roost communally until the breeding season returns. Then they once again become strongly territorial, often returning to their original nests. This accounts for the fact that sometimes you will see crows in large colonies; and at other times, they hover together in small family units, driving away outsiders, even other corvids. Perching pairs can be seen in that stage preening, cooing, and grooming each other. There is no way to tell a male crow from a female except by size (the male is larger with a thicker bill) and behavior (the female is less aggressive). The female lays the eggs and sits on them, and the male brings food to her and the chicks.

Crows in captivity have been known to live up to twenty years. Researchers believe they live even longer in the wild. Though they mate for life, they may occasionally cheat on one another, according to some of the humans who have observed them in a controlled environment.

Crows make a number of different sounds besides caw. Their mating call is an odd *gwong* sound. Ravens, we are told, make a deeper, more commanding *kwark* sound. There are other calls, some almost bell-like. Those who have studied crow talk claim they have a repertoire of fifteen to twenty long-distance calls, with an assortment of squawks, gargles, and coos that are used in intimate family situations. They have also been known to imitate certain sounds of human speech, especially in captivity.

Next to food, which represents every animal's most pressing search, the family unit is the crow's deepest interest. They are patient, devoted parents, even when the young are out of the nest and crying constantly to be fed. I marvel how the parents can put up with the incessant squawking of the youngsters, particularly after they are big enough to look for their own food.

My insight into crows is not based on scientific research. I am grateful to those who have done that. But even though we know more about crows today than ever before, we still do not know everything. As Bernd Heinrich said, "There is no substitute for direct observations, especially when you don't know what the relevant variables are." Meanwhile, as we study crows, you can be sure that they are just as busy studying us.

This bit of poetry has attempted to capture what happened to me that sunny morning when I heard a crow call my name. It is significant to me that the crow's cry should stir another one heard years ago when life was newer but no less profound.

The Crow That Spoke My Name

The crow that spoke my name today
Did not know, could not have known
That its call would unearth another time
When child I was, enchanted and alone,
Crept through a river meadow following
A killdeer with cries like tiny beads on stone.

Slowly I crawled on hands and knees,
Thinking because a wing dragged the ground
She had been injured, wanting me to know
The plight of one made to fly, now earthbound.
Through cropped grass she led me thus,
While I rejoiced to be the one she'd found.

As I reached out, suddenly she soared,
Disappearing into a broad, limitless sky.
The crafty thespian had led me from her nest
Where precious eggs lay hidden from my eye,
Left me standing at meadow's empty edge
With nothing but her triumphant cry.

I've stood in that same spot many times,
Waist-high in things beyond my grasp,
Wanting what was not mine to take,
Searching for the key that would unclasp.
Then a bold and noisy crow spoke my name
And bore my yearning spirit home at last.

Rodney R. Romney

Chapter Two

"Honey, Could You Watch the Kids Awhile?"

It soon became apparent to me that Charlie and Clarabelle lived in one of the tall firs that stood in the ravine at the edge of our yard. I noticed that when he had food in his beak, he would fly straight back to his nest, which was so well camouflaged I could hardly see it. I thought perhaps he was storing food for later use. Only later did I realize Charlie was carrying supplies to Clarabelle, who was sitting on the eggs. For at least a month, she was utterly dependent on Charlie for food. After the eggs had hatched, Charlie's visits would be met by hoarse cries as little scrawny necks shot up and little red mouths were opened to receive the food that Charlie would regurgitate into their waiting bills. I also learned that the nest was kept clean by the parents eating the feces of the nestlings and regurgitating it back into their ever-open bills. We humans might prefer not knowing that, but it is an efficient method.

When Clarabelle began to leave the nest, Charlie would be invited to babysit. One day he was sitting on a branch just outside the nest with little Clancy perched there beside him. Clancy, unsteady on his little thin legs, was obviously unhappy to be prodded out of the security of his nest and was squawking at Charlie with beak wide open. He wanted to be fed. Charlie endured this chatter for a while and then reached over with his head and rudely pushed little Clancy off the branch. Clancy screamed noisily as he began to plummet toward the ground. Eventually he found his wings and flew in a blind circle, trying to get back to the home tree, screaming every flap of the way. Charlie watched with no great concern, probably relieved to have a moment's respite from the little brat's eternal squawking. At length the chick got back to the branch where his father was sitting, where he crouched, shivering and whimpering with terror. As Clancy huddled next to his parent, Charlie suddenly flew off with no great show of concern for the fact that his little son had just been through the most terrifying experience of his young life.

Clancy clung to the branch for the next hour, shivering and sobbing softly. It seemed a cruel, hard way to learn a lesson, and a part of me wanted to scold Charlie for not being more gentle and patient. Another part of me wanted to crawl up on the tree limb and cuddle the poor little chick. But I also knew that Clancy had to learn who he was and what he had been given, if he was ever going to take care of himself.

It is the same for humans. As we mature, we must learn what powers we possess and how we can use these when they are needed. Like the baby crow, we often think we are helpless and dependent on others until the forces of life finally conspire to push us off our perch. Then in falling, we may discover we too can fly. It is, as Thoreau said, "Not until we are lost do we begin to find ourselves." And Herman Hesse reminds us, "Our only guide is our homesickness." Little Clancy pushed from his branch into a vast emptiness where he had never been before and, by the very one he had first learned to trust, reminds us that there is a secret turning in this life. It is this same secret that makes birds learn to fly, makes humans dare to explore, and helps the universe to turn.

Bernd Heinrich, who has unraveled many truths about the social habits of ravens in the northeastern part of the United States through painstaking research, believes that fledglings remain near the nest site for about three weeks, after which a kind of mutual estrangement takes place between parents and children. The young voluntarily leave and never return, while new young from other areas may come and take their place. Most raven researchers agree with Heinrich and say that these juveniles form into vagrant swarms, possibly akin to the teenage gangs, which our disinherited urban youth often form today. It is unclear if they remain in these gangs permanently or if they attach themselves to other flocks. It is unusual for crows to remain alone. They may scout and forage singly at times, but in the nonbreeding season, they will seek a communal, nocturnal roost. They seem to be designed for community. The reasons for this are several. It is easier for a community to fend off predators and to find food.

Here is one of the more fascinating facts about crows. While they may hunt individually, they will alert others to the presence of food. Someone in the flock usually acts as the dinner bell to call the others to eat. This may be a juvenile whose place in the flock is not yet fully established and who hopes thereby to gain favor. I have noticed that when a flock comes to feed, as opposed to a family, the larger older crows usually eat first. Smaller younger crows, who were the first to squawk "food," hang back, either from shyness or out of deference to the hierarchy.

It concerns me slightly that Charlie and Clarabelle can dispense of Clancy and Crista in such a casual and callous manner. Yet their parental dedication in those early weeks was intense and unfailing. Like all animals, they know the young carry the seeds for the future of the species, and they will do all they can to assure their safety and well-being up to a certain point in time. Once their young are on their way to adulthood, the parents not only kick them out of the nest, but the kids also seem to know when it is time to go. Whether they ever come back to the home nest to show off their kiddies to the grandparents is unlikely. The grandparents are too busy becoming parents all over again.

All creatures, regardless of the ways humans classify or treat them, represent something of God's purpose in action. Every living thing has a particular purpose and a function in the universal plan of life, and everything has a completeness and a perfection if we have the inner vision to see it.

On August 10, 2000, Valerie Reitman, staff writer for the *Los Angeles Times*, released a story about the "feathered terrorists of Tokyo." Roving bands of crows, she said, were harassing, attacking—apparently even stalking—the populace of Japan's largest city. According to her information, about twenty-one thousand jungle crows, which are indigenous to parts of Asia, have taken up residence in Tokyo, triple the number of fifteen years ago. Clearly the food supply is better in the city than in the wilds. Especially plentiful are the cemeteries where food, including vegetables and fruit, is often brought as a gift for ancestors and where those paying respects often light incense sticks. The crows have even been blamed for starting a forest fire when they picked up an incense stick and dropped it in a nearby stand of trees.

Documented accounts include a crow attacking a three-year-old girl who ran when she saw them swooping overhead. Her mother theorized that the birds sensed fear, which is why they attacked her daughter and not a little boy nearby who stood still when the crows rushed them. The girl was pecked on the head and was required to have tetanus shots.

In another incident, a political analyst was attacked by two crows on the roof of his Tokyo office building. He took off his belt and started swinging it. The birds kept their distance. But a few days later as this man arrived at work with some of his colleagues, hundreds of crows were waiting for them. They threatened the men by yelling and crying. Apparently they had alerted their friends and came back to promise revenge. Maybe they didn't like the man's politics.

Poisoning birds is prohibited in Tokyo, so in the spring of 2000, the city hired five extermination companies to take down nests and kill the chicks while they are in the nest. Parents of the chicks watched this horror from nearby trees. Altogether only sixty nests were destroyed, each of which contained two or three chicks, so the campaign could hardly be rated a success. But the damage done to the psyche of the parent crows, who witnessed the extermination of their dearest possessions, must have been intolerable. It is a small wonder that crows in Tokyo now rate humans as their most hated enemies.

It makes for a good news story to label crows as huge jet-black villains with intimidating beaks, killer claws, and a caw that sounds like a seagull on steroids. Though it was admitted the wounds on the three-year-old girl were superficial, much was made of the trauma and terror she continues to suffer (apparently she is the only casualty thus far). And who is to say that perhaps parent crows, who saw their own children slaughtered, were getting even in the only way they could—by attacking the children of the adults who had attacked them.

Ascribing human motives to animal behavior is always risky, and likewise judging animals by moral rules humans have established for themselves may not always work. But the truth is the borderline between the two is inevitably blurred. We humans have enormous advantages over animals. It is not realistic to portray the animals' world as invariably right, but the behavior pattern of parent to child is remarkably similar in all species. Watching Clancy and Crista quiver their wings in that dazzling, attention-getting motion and opening their mouths and begging for food was apparently irresistible to their parents. The parental instinct is innate in all creatures, *Corvus* as well as *Homo sapiens*, and the grief they feel at the destruction of their young is also common. Just as it is believed there is an aesthetic tendency in certain species (crows, for example, are attracted by straight lines more than bent ones and like shiny round objects rather than dull irregular ones), so there is a common concern that the young must survive. They carry the seeds of the future. Ira Progoff, psychologist and professor, said that animals not only strive to maintain their own lives, but they are also always ready to surrender their lives "in the service of a larger life continuity." An animal's true instinct "is not for *self*-preservation but for *life* preservation." We humans could perhaps learn a new and gentler ethic from animals.

In the late 1950s, crows everywhere began to migrate to cities where the food supply is better, a situation which we humans created by our increasing population and our encroachment on wilderness areas that once belonged to animals. Hiroshi Kawachi, deputy director of Tokyo's branch of the Japan Wild Bird Association, said that their problem with the crows was a result of the city's failure to adequately dispose of garbage. But why should we begrudge crows, or any living creature, the opportunity to survive from the scraps we no longer want? Can we not learn somehow to coexist with the animals of this world, who were here before we humans were and whose very presence in the environment makes it possible for us to be here as well? It is altogether possible that they provide some beneficial services in our communities and may have been blamed for some crimes that they themselves did not commit. Perhaps the more we interact with crows and other animals, and they with us, the more we will come to appreciate each other.

Scientists predict that, given current trends, the planet will lose at least a quarter of its species in the next fifty years, a change that could set off cascading ecological effects and lead to landscapes populated primarily by "weedy" species, such as rats, ragweed, and cockroaches. Human destruction of the earth is more to blame for our woes than anything else. So if you are lucky enough to have crows living near your home, why not try to get acquainted with them? You may be surprised at what they would teach you.

One day I met a little boy on the street in front of our house. He had a rock flipper in his hands and was scanning the trees for a target. I did not know him, but I felt I could not pass up the opportunity that was before me. "Have you seen Charlie Crow?" I asked. He looked at me somewhat stupidly, and I hurried on, "He usually comes here to be fed, but perhaps he doesn't know you and is too shy to show himself. Would you like to stay and meet him?"

He shook his head and started on down the street. "He is a very wise bird," I called after him. "He has something to share with you if you are willing to get acquainted. Come back again, and I will introduce you to him." I watched him tuck the flipper in his pocket. I could only hope he would open his heart to a kinder way to treat animals than to make targets out of them. If children can become receptive to the values that animals want to share with them, they will start to discover the universal heartbeat that pervades and unites all life into one.

The Sufi mystic and poet Rumi said,

Something opens our wings,
Something makes boredom and hurt disappear.
Someone fills the cup in front of us.
We taste only sacredness.

The way of love is not
a subtle argument.
The door there
is devastation.
Birds make great sky-circles
of their freedom.
How do they learn it?
They fall, and falling,
they're given wings.

The Essential Rumi, translations by Coleman Barks with John Moyne (San Francisco, Harper, 1995) p. 243.

Chapter Three

You Cannot Fool a Crow!

If there is a crow anywhere in your vicinity, no matter where you are, you can count on knowing that crow is watching you. This is due in part to the fact that nearly all birds have amazing vision, and the crow is no exception. Along with powerfully keen eyesight comes a superhuman memory, clear problem-solving skills, and an inordinate curiosity. But the greatest gift of crows is the magnificence of their minds. These birds have amazing brainpower, which leads them to be both wary and interested in human beings and to exhibit certain characteristics that seem sometimes a mimicry of our own.

I watched Charlie first carry food to his nest to feed Clarabelle and their fledglings. But one day, after several trips back and forth, he began to bury his food in the soft soil of my rose garden. Two days later, I observed him scratching in the dirt and extracting the food he had hidden. Later I saw him soak hard bread in water to make it softer, and I watched him hold a peanut down with one foot while using his bill to open the shell. A walnut gave him greater difficulty, so he soared above the road and dropped it on the pavement. If it did not break apart in the falling, he would leave it there and wait for a car to come by in the hope it might crush the nut for him. He adores peanuts, but he also enjoys having me throw them in the air so he can dive for them. He takes peculiar pleasure in catching them before they hit the ground. None of the other crows behave with such unrestrained antics. Only Charlie. Sometimes I wonder if he might have been raised in captivity since he seems to have less fear of humans than do his companions.

Whenever I leave the house for my morning walk, Charlie is generally in a nearby tree. He has some sort of built-in radar system regarding time that is more accurate than my wristwatch. If I am late, he calls me. If I come out of the house carrying food in my pocket or tucked out of sight in my jacket, he knows that I have it even though he cannot see it, and the word goes out to all, "He has food." By his call, he summons a small colony of anywhere from six to a dozen other crows who congregate with him in the trees. I have a particular bank where I feed them, and their excitement intensifies as I walk toward that spot. They dance on the branches, calling enthusiastically and often pooping spontaneously, as though they are too excited to hold back. Only once did I become the recipient of their deposit—when a white streak of excrement fell on my arm. As I stopped to wipe it away, everything became strangely silent. I had the feeling there was a newcomer in the group that day, one that had not learned the drill—the drill being that you don't crap on the one who feeds you. The silence carried a strange feeling of remonstration against the offender and an implied concern lest I be offended. Since that day, it has never happened again to me. Crows defecate constantly and keep their nests clean by eating the feces of their young. Our driveway and patio are sometimes spattered with what I refer to as their "calling cards," a fact which Beverly, my wife, finds more bothersome than I do.

If I leave the house, whether to walk up to the mailbox or to get in my car to leave, Charlie has this eerie sense of knowing that the routine is now different. He watches me just as intently, but he is silent. He knows I have other business to carry out. When I return, even if I have been away for several days, he again has an intuitive sense of my arrival and will nearly always be somewhere in the vicinity to call out a greeting.

But as Bernd Heinrich, behavioral ecologist, reminds us, we should not judge an animal by its relationship with humans but by its own right and its own intrinsic value. They will show us as much of themselves as we are prepared to receive.

Some writers who have studied crows have drawn the conclusion that they are basically bored. Like the gifted child who must endure the elementary routines of his own age-group, crows find themselves insufficiently challenged and, as a consequence, fall into the role of tricksters and troublemakers. Many who have studied the habits of crows believe when they are given social value and human attention, which they crave, they cease being predators of other birds. It is my personal belief that crows only become nest predators as a last resort, in the same way that humans will resort to cannibalism if faced with starvation.

Their food preferences seem to be seasonally influenced. Charlie and crew love bread containing raisins and seeds, but their eagerness wanes if there is no variety. I regularly offer them bread (purchased from a bakery that sells day-old goods at a discount) and supplement it with table scraps, cereals, rice, and a variety of vegetables and berries. Once I brought home fish-and-chips from a deli and gave the portion we did not eat to the crows. I kid you not,

I actually saw one of them dip a french fry in catsup and then drag a portion of the fish through the tartar sauce that had been left on the plate.

About once a week, when we have pancakes, they seem to know it and wait eagerly in the trees for their share. I usually break the pancakes into bite-size pieces so there will be enough to go around. Once, when I did not, I watched a crow carefully cut the pancake into strips with his beak so he could stockpile and carry more of it away. How crows feed depends on whether there are fledglings and a mate waiting in the nest for delivery of the groceries. The priority at such times for the male crow is not to satisfy his own hunger but to take care of the little family that is depending on him to come home with the bacon.

You also cannot fool a crow as to your intentions or your moods, and they refuse to be pawns. One time two students from the University of Washington, who had heard about my penchant for crows, called and asked if they could come out and film my feeding them as a project for a class in photography. They arrived early and quietly concealed themselves out of sight so they would not frighten the crows by their presence. That morning not a single crow showed up, even though I spread the bank with fresh, warm pancakes and called to them with my usual clucking noises. All the time the students were there until they drove out of the yard two hours later, no crows appeared nor were any even heard. Once the students had given up and left, the crows magically appeared out of nowhere to consume the food I had strewn. They knew what was going on but refused to participate in it.

Usually crows are not timid, but something, perhaps the presence of strangers carrying video cameras that might have looked like guns or trapping equipment, prevented them from becoming film stars that day. Maybe crows are just clever comedians, who decided that day to play a trick on us and show us who was in charge.

Someone who is also a *corviphile* told me that the crows near his home forage only on the bicycle lanes so as to avoid traffic. On one-way streets, they know the traffic patterns and are alert to the only direction from which cars will approach. He wondered if crows can read and concluded perhaps they do it better than some drivers.

I probably tend to anthropomorphize crows a little too much. I am not interested in making crows look like people. I am interested in learning from them what I think would be helpful in establishing better relations with them and with nature in general. It is to our advantage that we do this.

Earlier I said that after young birds leave their nests, they create new families and don't return. Dr. Carolee Caffrey of Oklahoma State University has a different theory. Netting crows and tagging them, she was able to watch one female crow, who had established her own nest, fly more than a mile to visit her parents every other Friday afternoon. "She'd hang around with them for about an hour," said Caffrey. "She did it for years." (Reported in *Country Journal*, July/August 1998 in an article by Cynthia Berger.) It is logical to assume if crows mate for life, they will also retain lifetime relationships and affection for each other.

Although most of us cannot tell one crow from another, clearly their sense of recognition, along with their eyesight and intuition, is much greater than our own. Perhaps their sense of fidelity is also greater than ours. Whether we admire them or think there are far too many of the rascals, the fact remains they have been with us a long time and will probably never make an endangered species list.

Crows are also brave. I watched them one morning take swipes at a blue heron who had swept into their territory, possibly to do a little nest hunting for himself. Seven or eight crows took after the heron and drove him away. Once a seagull wandered up from the beach below our house and swooped down on the bank where I was feeding the crows. At that moment, only two crows were eating, and they beat a swift retreat. Had there been more crows, they might have challenged the gull, but I got the distinct feeling the two crows feeding realized they were no match for this much-larger bird, at least not without backup.

Despite their reputation for having omnivorous natures, I have never seen crows attack smaller birds. In fact, when I spread birdseed on the bank, the crows tolerate the presence of smaller birds joining in the feast.

I did witness a fight in a tree between a squirrel and two crows. The squirrel had apparently approached the nest, perhaps to steal an egg or a chick, and the parents drove it off. No one was hurt, but the commotion around that little skirmish was startling.

Life preying on life is one of the hard facts of nature, and while we might wish it were different, we need to remember that humans are the greatest offenders in that regard. Our penchant for killing animals, sometimes just for the pleasure of it, has made the human the most feared creature in the animal world. When a wild animal decides to trust a human, it requires overcoming centuries of fear and mistrust. And who knows? Maybe as crows learn to trust humans and as humans learn to respect crows, the crows will stop harassing other birds and creatures around them. Maybe we humans are the key to the earth's call to restore relationships.

Th' Only Good Crow's a Dead Crow

He spoke the words aloud several times,
as though he liked the taste of them in his mouth,
then went on to explain his reasons:
"They multiply faster 'n rabbits,
squawk from mornin' till night,
crap like cream cheese out a water hose,
mess up streets and yards and cars,
an' eat dead things 'long the roadside."

I silently reviewed each of his arguments:
Counted up the progeny he had spawned,
Reviewed his perennial need to complain,
Thought of the litter in his backyard,
And wondered what he had eaten for dinner
if not some dead thing, carved and cooked,
involuntarily surrendering its life
so he, the overlord, could stay alive.

"Ya see one crow, you've seen 'em all."
He went on, satisfied I was still listening.
"I've seen 'em ruin entire fields of corn.
No matter where you go, you'll see a crow.
If it was 'lowed, I'd reduce the population."
He aimed an imaginary rifle into the trees,
Smirking as he repeated his mantra,
"Th' only good crow's a dead crow."

What is there to say to such a one?
He's right on every count, you know.
His mistake is separating a crow from himself,
doesn't know he is looking into a mirror,
can't realize that what we see around us
is the same as we see within.
Crow doesn't care—deep down he knows
that he is the strong muscle of the world.

Rodney R. Romney

Chapter Four

Whose Line Is It Anyway?

A program on television titled *Whose Line Is It Anyway?* invites participants to act out roles that are given to them by the host or the audience. As I have indicated, crows are great mimics and will often imitate human behavior and speech. Crows are represented both positively and negatively in the legends and myths that have been developed about them down through the ages. At Charlie's suggestions, I want to review a few of those ancient stories. But first, let me point out that baby crows learn the same way that human babies learn—from the example of their parents.

Crista, daughter of Clancy and Claribelle, accompanied them one morning to *les petit dejeuner a la bistro sur la banque* (breakfast at the café on the bank, for the linguistically challenged). She stayed demurely behind her parents until the meal had been served; then when the waiter (I) had retreated, she flew down to join the noisy group of diners. It was amusing to observe her. She approached a peanut warily, danced up to it from one side, then backed up, and approached it from another before backing away. After several futile forays, she finally retreated to her branch where she called out her frustrations. Clearly she was saying, "I want the peanut, I want the peanut, *I am afraid of the peanut.*" Crista would only learn to overcome her fears and scramble for her portions of the meal by observing the actions of her parents. Crows, like humans, learn their lines from observing the behavior of their elders.

In a similar way, we humans have learned our lines about crows from the myths and traditions of our ancestors and, in the process, have learned something about ourselves. These stories represent the prominence the crow has played in the development of human thought.

René Descartes, the French philosopher who lived from 1596 to 1650, suffered severely from congenital myopia in his early adult years. As his physical vision blurred, so did his inward vision. Feeling socially shy and awkward, he began to avoid all social contacts. He often spent his days sitting on a park bench, despondently talking to himself and feeding sandwich crumbs to pigeons. A crow observed this and one day landed on the bench, so close to the brooding Descartes that the man could visually make out the bird's form. Piteously, he called out, "Crow, Crow, is it all a cruel illusion?"

The crow, after consuming the last of the crumbs, replied coldly, "I think not," and flew off.

The visually impaired and depressed Descartes suddenly felt his mind leap forward in a new direction. He jumped from the bench, shouting, "But I do think! Therefore I am!" With this visitation from the crow, Descartes began to experience a new sense of well-being, located a competent optometrist who enabled him to see again, and founded the Age of Reason. Whether factual or fictional, the crow became known as *cognitum non* and is enshrined in legend as the Cartesian crow.

In Greek/Roman mythology, ravens and crows were white; until one day, a crow brought bad news to the god Apollo and was consequently turned black. Since then, the crow has always been viewed as a messenger, whose greatest attribute was watchfulness. In China a three-legged sun crow was worshiped as a symbol of solitude. The Athapaskan Indians of Alaska believed the crow was the creator of the world. The crow was also associated with creation in the early stories of the Celts. In the Norse tradition, the god Odin had two ravens who were his messengers, and the prophet Elijah in the Hebrew scriptures was fed by ravens and crows while he was hiding in the wilderness.

To this day, crows are symbols of creation and spiritual strength. My grandfather used to tell me if you ever found a feather from a crow, it would bring you good luck. He claimed to have learned this from the Indians. As a result, whenever I see a crow feather, even today, I am impelled to pick it up and keep it with me. Many people believe today that crows are messengers who remind us that creation and magic are available to us every day.

Not all crow legends are positive. In the near East, the raven or crow was considered unclean because it is a scavenger. It is one of the foods listed as forbidden in the Hebrew Bible. The raven was sent forth by Noah after the flood but failed to return to the ark, a mission that was later accomplished by the dove. During the Middle Ages, the croak of the raven was believed to foretell a death or the loss of a battle, and it was even taught to early Christians that wicked priests were turned into ravens when they died.

The Yakima tribe in eastern Washington shows how animals embody the traits of trickery and vanity that often characterize humans in the following legend.

Fighting monsters and making the world ready for people was a hard and tiring job. As Coyote made his way across the Cascade Mountains and into Puget Sound territory, he became ravenously hungry. He stood beneath a high cliff and looked up. Above him, he saw Crow with a ball of deer fat in his mouth. Coyote looked at Crow and thought about how good the food would taste and then wondered how to get the fat for himself. He thought for a while then laughed. He knew what he would do.

Coyote called up to Crow. "Oh, Chief," he said, "you are good and so wise, and your good, pleasing voice is famous throughout the land. I know you are a big chief. Let me hear your voice. I want to hear you, Chief Crow."

Crow was flattered that Coyote had called him Chief. He answered him, "Caw."

"Oh, Chief Crow," Coyote replied, "your 'caw' wasn't much. I know that you can sing better than that, for I have heard the stories of your beautiful voice. You can sing a good, loud song for me. I want to hear you, loud and strong."

Crow was pleased and obliged Coyote. He opened his mouth wide and called from the cliff as loud as he could, "C-A-A-A-W!"

With that, the ball of fat fell from his mouth. Coyote snatched it quickly and laughed,

"You are not a wise chief," Coyote told Crow. "In fact, you aren't even a chief at all—you fell for my trick. I wanted your deer fat because I am hungry. Now you can go hungry because of your foolishness."

The intent of these legends is to tell us that good and evil come in the same package. You learn from both. Crow, one of the most frequently used characters in the ancient stories, is not only the source of things gone awry but also the one who eventually straightens things out. Also the nature of the crow varies from culture to culture. The Eskimo crow may serve in the shaman role; while in Siberia, the crow takes on a kind of slapstick, comedic persona.

In the Pacific Northwest, the crow is generally regarded as the one who brings life and order. It is believed Crow stole the sunlight from the one who wanted to keep the world in darkness. Crow is honored in Native American art and is often placed on totem poles as one who can help you shape your life into better directions and who has the knowledge to teach you how to speak the languages of other animals. Crow is also associated with winter and the winter solstice, the shortest and the darkest day of the year. From that day forth, the light shines a little more each day. This is symbolic of the influence of Crow. Crow teaches us how to go into the dark and bring forth new light. With each trip in, we develop the ability to bring more light out. This is the kind of mythology that can enhance the wisdom and spiritual understanding of all.

One legend from the Northwest Coast Indians tells of a cruel trick Raven played on Mama Crow and her hungry babies when he exchanged the seal meat she had in her basket for stones. In this legend, it is the raven and not the crow who represents trickery, though they are both from the same family.

Animals become cultural heroes in some traditions, but they usually reflect the good as well as the bad characteristics of humans. They help us see ourselves and teach us how to live properly in this world. So though Crow often played tricks on people, was regarded as the source of things gone awry, and had an insatiable appetite for mischief and pranks, he also brought the essentials for existence—food, fire, clothing, and shelter.

Ancient legends deal with more than just animals. They tell us that everything, all creatures and even the land, has spirit. A spiritual connection exists between people, animals, and the land. The balance of relationships is difficult to maintain in our growing technological culture, but these relationships are as imperative today as they were when the legends and myths were formed.

I have not read this in print, but I heard a story about the Dalai Lama, the spiritual and political leader of Tibetan Buddhism, who was forced to flee his native Tibet in 1959 when it was occupied by China. During their flight, it has been claimed by these exiles that they were safely guided by a flock of ravens, which stayed with them and led them safely across the border.

I have no story to match that, but I do recall a time in my life a few years ago when I was struggling with depression and wondering how I would be able to go on. I came home one afternoon after a session with a therapist, and there in the driveway, I found seven crow feathers. Tell me there had been a crow fight. Tell me it was the molting season, and crows were just getting rid of feathers that day. Tell me whatever you wish. All I can tell you is that when I picked up those feathers, I had a wonderful sensation of being cared for and understood, greater than anything I had felt in a long time. The feathers still sit on a window ledge in my study, symbols of a dark time when I was finally able to find the light. If Charlie and his flock could do that for me, what other response than gratitude and love should I have for them? That day they were literally, for me, the messengers who promised I would come through the darkness into greater light.

The Gift

A bird flew against one of our windows and fell instantly to the patio.
She had mistaken the reflection in the glass for a valley of sunlight.
She lay quiet, eyes glazed. I picked her up and carried her to the edge
Of the yard, near the wide expanse of sky she had been seeking.

I sat down and released the tiny body from my hands to the quiet grass,
Returning her to the good and gentle earth from which she had arisen.
Then I noticed light slipping back into her eyes. She blinked a few times.
Stroking her back, I prayed for energy to come and lift her into freedom.

Like a priest, performing an ancient ritual, I offered the chalice of light
And the bread of healing to this stunned creature lying in my chapel.
Followed a moment's hesitation, then fire seemed to creep into her frame.
She moved her head, heaving tiny shuddering feathers against my touch.

I lifted my hands. Her wings quivered. Suddenly she rose into the air.
At that exact moment, my cat bounded toward us with anxious mewing.
We watched the bird disappear into the sky—cat reluctantly, I gratefully.
With every beat of her wings, she was proclaiming, "I have my life back."

I know what it is to strike against a glass wall and lie stunned and afraid,
Wondering if light will shine again, if forgiveness can ever be offered.
I also know what it is to rise into shimmering and glorious freedom.
There is no greater peace than the place of loving again what you are.

I fear no more the cold gray voices that would place me in the dome of dark,
For I have come out from that dome into the circle of love enough times
To know, with the bird, that the comforting hand that first holds, then frees,
Can never be defeated. I too know what it is to have my life given back.

Rodney R. Romney

Chapter Five

"Can't We All Just Get Along?"

The plaintive cry of Rodney King, an African-American man, arrested and beaten savagely a few years ago by police in Los Angeles, is the lament growing out of our failed racial relations and the disturbing heart cry of creation.

"Can't we all just get along?" could be part of the message that crows have traditionally brought to the earth and are still trying to impart. If the ancient legends we briefly scanned in the previous chapter tell us anything at all, it is that the traditional role of crows as messengers needs to be heeded today. They may be telling us something about our human activities that are preventing creation from getting along.

John Marzluff, assistant professor of Wildlife Science at the University of Washington, wrote an article in *Earthcare* (September 1999), a publication of the Seattle Audubon Society, in which he suggested crows are playing out their role as messengers by telling humans today to (1) support growth management and urban infill so we reduce sprawl and its associated toll on relatively intact habitats; (2) encourage developers and homeowners to leave native vegetation around homesites; (3) demand that our local and regional land-use planners provide wildlife habitat in addition to human habitat; and (4) to recreate responsibly so that we do not fuel populations of nest predators, including crows. Says Marzluff, "The next time you see a crow gulp down a robin's egg or mob a raptor, refrain from shooting the messenger and reflect instead on the message." Crows may be getting the blame for crimes that humans have committed against them.

Is it irresponsible for humans to feed crows, as I have done in recent years? The question is legitimate and needs to be considered, in light of the fact that the leftovers I spread for the crows may possibly fuel the crow population in an area that is already overpopulated. I can only answer that question from what I have observed.

First, I am not the crows' main source of food in my neighborhood. What I give them could only be classified as a midmorning snack at best and not a very substantial one at that.

Second, I have not noticed any significant increase of the crows around my home in the last five years. The population varies, as it does in all areas, from the nesting period to the communal roosting period. The communal period I liken to political conventions, when crows within a geographic area get together to exchange information, relay any unusual developments, and make decisions about hierarchy. The crows which come to my bank and feed are never more than a dozen and often less. I believe they are the descendants of Charlie and Clarabelle and their extended family. Some of the fledglings may leave the family dynasty and join a new one, while others may choose to remain in the area.

Third, I believe the crows relate to me as more than the jolly giant grocer. They are not stupid, and they are not underachievers. They are possibly dissatisfied with the narrow margins of their lives. Whether they are the world's smartest birds, as some ornithologists have announced, or ambitious understudies waiting for a break, they are excessively bright and insatiably curious about many things, including me and my routine. Their homelife is stable and secure; they are ruled by monogamous relationships, and their actions toward family members are tender and protective. I am the variable that offers them a break from what is often an otherwise monotonous existence. I give them, in essence, a new playmate.

I have seldom seen crows fight each other. Once they drove off a vagrant crow who had come to feed with them and who obviously did not belong. But for the most part, they are amicable and entirely willing to share the bounty wherever and whenever it is offered.

Something else has happened that has been interesting to observe, and that is the interaction that has developed between the crows and the squirrels that jointly claim my little piece of real estate as part of their territory. Our home sits on a bluff about thirty feet above the Puget Sound, offering a sweeping view of the Sound and the Olympic Mountains to the west. A small ravine, which is really a greenbelt, runs along the edge of our property line. A little creek flows through the ravine and gurgles its way down the hillside and into the Sound. The ravine is heavily wooded, but the tallest trees have been trimmed so that they frame the water view rather than hinder it. These are the trees where Charlie and family live. In these trees also live a number of squirrels. Higher in the greenbelt can be found mountain beavers, raccoons, and possums, but these are seldom seen in our yard. The squirrel population of the ravine closest to our house is equal to the crow population, limited, I calculate, to one or two families.

One day I observed a squirrel digging up some bulbs that I had just planted in my flower garden. I am willing to allow my yard to be a wildlife refuge, but I also enjoy having flowers. I decided to hang a squirrel feeder on one of the trees and see if I could direct their search away from the garden to the tree. It worked. Within a short time, the squirrels found the feeder, which I filled with peanuts; and from then on, they left the garden alone, except occasionally using it as a place to bury nuts.

The crows were frantic that the feeder contained nuts, which the squirrels could reach but they could not. Although they worked furiously with their beaks, leaving deep grooves in the wood and scratches in the clear plastic, they were simply not constructed to be able to lift the top of the feeder with their heads and reach in and extract the nuts, which they could see from the outside. After watching their frustration and seeing them trying to drive the squirrels away, it occurred to me that I needed to feed all of them at the same time. So when I filled the squirrel feeder, I also spread a few nuts on the ground for the crows. This ended the warfare. One day, when I was running late and had to be downtown for an appointment, I took the crows' bread and the squirrels' nuts and threw them down on the ground together. As I was driving out, I looked back and saw that not only were the squirrels and crows eating side by side, a gull had also joined them. No one was chasing anyone else away. When there is enough food for everyone, there is no more need to battle. It is true for all species.

A situation developed among the squirrels that was not lost on the crows. One squirrel, which came regularly to the feeder, was pregnant. Her swollen furry sides gave evidence she was about to give birth. After a brief absence, she showed up at the feeder, looking somewhat gaunt and with nipples protruding from her white underbelly. She would take only one nut and scamper back into the ravine with it. She was as regular as a housewife at a food market, except she was now shopping for more than just herself. A period of time went by and one day she came to the feeder, displaying a huge circular wound running across her neck and down her back. It was as though some larger animal had clamped its jaws around her body. She moved with difficulty. Securing several nuts from the feeder and storing them in her mouth, she then left. A few days later, she was back, but this time she had two little ones in tow. The feeder was empty at the time, so she waited expectantly, looking toward the house for my appearance, with the little ones crouched behind her. They looked like three little Buddha statues in meditation. She did not run away when she saw me emerge but waited patiently as I filled the feeder. The wound looked festered and ugly, and I wished there was something I could do for her. She crawled up to the feeder somewhat slowly, lifted the lid with her head, and extracted a nut. The little ones followed her example. After eating for a while, they loaded nuts into their jaws and left.

It was the last time I saw the little mother squirrel. I suspect she died shortly thereafter from her wounds. Her final act was to give her babies to me to take care of. Because they had not learned to fear humans, they soon became like little pets, scampering toward me when they saw me coming, sitting on their haunches, and waiting for the peanut to be dropped onto the ground in front of them or into their outstretched paws.

The crows were silent witnesses to this new development. While I never saw any outer evidence of sympathy on the part of the crows and also knew they would not have been above eating the carcass of the dead mother squirrel if they could have found it, there seemed to be a collective mute assent on their parts that the baby squirrels should be protected and cared for. So they watched closely my feeding of them and their attachment to me.

There is compassion at every level of creation. I am convinced of it. It is planted within every living thing by the Great Constructor of the universe. Once the basic needs for survival have been assured and once tenderness has somewhere been shown, if only briefly, then compassion is somehow released and allowed to come forth to touch everyone and everything. In that hallowed touch, we waken to our true being.

> **When despair for the world grows in me**
> **and I wake in the night at the least sound**
> **in fear of what my life and my children's lives may be,**
> **I go and lie down where the wood drake**
> **rests in his beauty on the water, and the great heron feeds.**
> **I come into the peace of wild things**
> **who do not tax their lives with forethought**
> **of grief. I come into the presence of still water.**
> **And I feel above me the day-blind stars**
> **waiting with their light. For a time**
> **I rest in the grace of the world, and am free.**

From "The Peace of Wild Things" in *Collected Poems* by Wendell Berry, North Point Press, San Francisco, CA, 1987.

Chapter Six

Even Crows Weep

Neighbors on our street, who have a lot about the size of an acre, had fifty-four trees cut down on their property. The outcry and anguish of the crows was deafening. They flew to neighboring trees and literally sobbed their despair over the loss of their habitat. "Let them build their nests in other trees," scoffed a realist neighbor. Yes, they can do that, as long as we don't cut down all the trees. But are we so insensitive as to think that crows may not develop attachment to their arboreal homes in the same way we humans get connected to our dwelling places? Charlie and Clarabelle have lived in the same tree in the ravine near our yard for as long as I have known them, and who knows how long before that? They have probably raised dozens of chicks in that nest. I can only draw the conclusion that to have that tree suddenly disappear would uproot their lives terribly.

A newspaper article advised homeowners if crows nest in the trees near their house, one of the options is to cut down the trees. Perhaps my neighbors read that article. I would suggest that instead of doing that, we get to know the crows. Once we do that, we will not only learn more about them, but we will also learn something about ourselves. One of the critical mandates in the Hebrew scriptures is that we all learn to coexist with nature. That indeed was the first assignment of Adam and Eve in the mythical Garden of Eden.

Crows live in trees for a number of reasons, the primary one being safety. Just as young crows imprint readily on whoever feeds them (usually their parents), they also develop an attachment to their home nest and their early surroundings. Some argue that their nests are not homes, just temporary structures. That may be true for the young birds, and it may even be true that some adult crows rebuild their nests every year. There is a lot we don't know about crows. All I can tell you is that in over the five years I have known Charlie and Clarabelle, they have kept the same nest. How do I know Charlie and Clarabelle apart from other crows? I only know them by their behavior toward me, which is distinctive in a number of ways.

Most crows have crossed a behavioral threshold and have adjusted to living in cities, as well as with the alterations that humans have created in the remaining wilderness areas. But this is not to say they are without feelings, and those feelings are often expressed in their vocal outpourings.

Crows, like other birds and animals, understand their part in the natural order, and nearly all of them have the ability to scratch out a living under tough conditions. They usually post a sentinel in the area to alert the others of danger or the presence of food. One of the first things most crows will do with food is to return with it to their nests, where it will be shared with the family. In that respect, they are like humans.

Nature itself is not always friendly. House cats are generally detested by crows. That is not because cats are a menace to the crows or their nests. It is because they are a menace to the small-bird population, much more so than the crows, and hence, they upset the balance of nature. John Marzluff, professor of Science at the University of Washington, argues that crows are not the reason that songbirds often fare poorly in urban areas. In fact, crows help songbirds by warning them of stalking cats and other predators. Mice, rats, and cats, both domestic and feral, are probably greater nest predators than crows.

My house cat, named Orange Roughy, refuses to go out in the yard when the crows are making a noise. If she is out and hears them cawing, she immediately wants to be inside. I suspect they are scolding her. When from inside the house she sees crows foraging for insects and worms on the lawn, she will twitch her tail and make mewing noises in her throat, but that's the limit of her interaction with crows. A smaller bird in the yard would send her to the door demanding to be released, but the crow reinforces her gratitude that she is house cat.

Crows will sometimes form a dislike against certain people and may even attack them. This happens more frequently when the chicks are coming out of the nests. Sometimes it happens for no reason that we can tell. But as I said earlier, you cannot fool a crow. Perhaps they can sense the person's disposition or intentions are not honorable. On the other hand, it could be that certain crows are just plain cantankerous, same as certain humans.

Once at the downtown church in Seattle, where I was a pastor for twenty years, a young crow fell into a stairwell near the front entrance and was unable to get out because of a wing injury. The lament of the crows around that stairwell was deafening during my sermon, which occasioned the congregation with much laughter since they knew of my propensity for crows but did not know why the birds were crying. At one point, I paused in my sermon and called out to them, "Quiet down. I'll be out in a minute."

After church was out, a dear woman who also loves crows rescued the baby from its trap and took it to a wildlife refuge on the outskirts of the city. Its injury was diagnosed as minor but required treatment and recuperation time, after which it would be released back into the wild. The adult crows lamented at the stairwell for several days following the loss of their little one. I often hoped it might come back to its family at the church, but its chances of doing that are probably impossible, given its age and the distance it was transported.

John Strachan, a filmmaker and friend from Bainbridge Island, sent me this delightful story of a crow he rescued. He called it "Something to Crow About." It is reprinted here with his permission.

> *Even as I whiz by at 40 miles per hour, I can see that the crow walking the centerline is going to fail the sobriety test. Rolling his eyes at my car, he holds shiny black wings out like a tightrope walker's umbrella, staggering sideways. Then in my rear view mirror I see him fall off the flat yellow line, plopping down, feathers askew in the middle of the oncoming traffic. This crow is soon to be a dead pigeon.*
>
> *Pulling off on the shoulder, I climb out to take a look. Close inspection reveals caramel glazed eyes that look like this crow has done ten rounds with Mohammed Ali. He's alive and breathing, but there is no intelligent connection with the present. This is the hit-and-run victim of a head-on with two tons of steel, the one time a crow didn't jump clear "just in time."*
>
> *And now another car is looming up in the lane occupied by the reeling bird. Black feathers are about to fly. When I reach down to pick up the bird, he scoots sideways, sidling along in an old vaudeville soft shoe, working his way diagonally across the lane to the shoulder, wings fluttering uselessly. And when I follow, he summons the energy to make one giant leap across a drainage ditch, landing wings splayed in the tall grass. There he eyes me balefully, unable to make another move but daring me to leap across the deep ditch to his resting place.*
>
> *It's a wide ditch. My junior high school long jump years are half a century behind me. The bird will probably be fine. Or die.*
>
> *Four hours later on my return trip home I can't resist the temptation to find out the best (or worst) news. Stopping the car, I cross the drainage ditch.*

Jeremiah (I had now named him) sat lopsided, exactly as I had left him—wings outstretched, seemingly unable to move, but looking me right in the eye. If ever I was going to see a "don't-just-stand-there-do-something" look, this was it. I tried to turn away but Jeremiah wasn't having any of it. He leaned his head to the side and cawed at me "Soooo?"

Walking a half block down the highway, I found a fording place and crossed the ditch. When I reached Jeremiah, he doesn't move as I take off my Husky sweatshirt and bend down, folding his wings carefully to his body, wrapping him up. He's in trouble and he knows it.

I drive to a nearby veterinarian only to be told, "No birds." I will have to go to Kingston, 25 miles away. But as I turn to leave, a young woman in medical "greens" comes out of the back and sees me holding Jeremiah.

"This is Suzy, our Vet Tech," the receptionist offers.

"That bird has been letting you carry him around like that?" she asks me.

"This crow has been bashed by one of us, and is now seeking redress," I reply.

"Could be all messed up inside," she says.

"I believe he's just a little dingy . . . and knows it."

"If he's in shock and stays out all night, I doubt if he'll make it." She is now stroking the bird's head. Jeremiah, sensing he needs to make a good impression, tilts his head, cooing softly, "Caahh."

"Hypothermia?" I ask.

"Uhuh," she answers.

Jeremiah squawks.

"We'll make a bed for him in a cage in the back, and if I can get him to come around, we'll get a little water down, may some food. He's got a chance." She takes bird and sweatshirt, heading for the back, ignoring the receptionist's, "We don't take birds."

Before I leave I see Jeremiah get wrapped up in a blanket and plumped down on a pillow, heater nearby, toasty warm. A cat in the next cage looks peeved, obviously another of the "we don't take birds" legion. But Jeremiah is happy. He looks at me through the cage bars, tilting his head. It's clear he's saying, "Thank you."

Funny how a crow can get to you. Hard to leave him.

The veterinarian returned my call the next day to tell me Jeremiah came around in the morning. After feeding him they had a releasing ceremony and applauded as he zoomed off, headed south in the direction I had brought him from. I may look him up.

Thanks, John, for a delightful and true story. And now one more which is not so delightful but which is a vivid example of crows weeping. It happened in my own neighborhood one morning when I was walking. A baby crow fell from its nest into the street and was hit by a passing truck and killed. Immediately a large group of crows gathered around its carcass and set up a deafening cacophony of sound. Because the baby was in the middle of the street, their mourning was interrupted by cars coming and going. I was walking by when this happened. I picked up the dead chick and carried it to a grassy spot away from the road. The crows followed; and as I withdrew, they again descended and gathered around the body, filling the air with their keening and wailing. This went on for the rest of the day. When Beverly came home from school that afternoon, the crows were still there. It was not just the parents who were weeping, it was a community of nearly two dozen who came to share in the loss.

Do crows weep? Of course they do. Anything that has the capacity to love also has the capacity to grieve when that love is lost or destroyed.

I am not an advocate of capturing crows and raising them in captivity. I think we do great damage to wild birds when we do this to them. But I am a passionate advocate of learning to understand God's presence in all creation and to treat all forms of life with as much reverence as we are capable. Just as persons congregate into communities and are bound to certain ecosystems, so are all forms of life. When we humans can reach beyond our own interests and rethink our attitudes and intentions toward nature and all its creatures, the greater will be our adventure. The more we interact compassionately and reverently with other species, the more we will appreciate each other and learn to coexist peacefully.

Crow's Nest

Brash but weary, they return at night
To the giant tree, green and upright,
With arms outspread, stretching, reaching
To these dark apostles, tirelessly teaching.

Silent now as stars, they claim their home
On vaulted beams, a sculptured throne,
Wherein they find their quiet place,
And rest in arms of generous grace.

They nestle, raven life together,
Neck on bill, claw on feather,
Their benediction gently said
O'er all the living and all the dead.

First light of dawn, from sleep released,
They fly on sun and soar on breeze,
Their watchful eyes scan earth amazed
They cry a psalm: O light, be praised!

We should not know them half as well
Were not they always glad to tell
They are the advent we await,
Their wings may open heaven's gate.

Rodney R. Romney

Chapter Seven

Crow Man

Carlos Castaneda was a popular writer in the 1960s, whose search for an inner reality that would result in living more fully in the outer world appealed to many in my generation and younger, who were then delving into higher education or starting life careers. We resonated with his idea of "not-doing," and we were drawn to his concept of a guru or shaman of some sort who would show us how to apprehend spirit in our lives. I look back on that period in my life with some amusement but also with appreciation. It taught me many important things and in some ways strengthened the foundation of my spiritual world on which I am still building today.

Castaneda claimed that the world, for all its differences of perception, has its own inner logic, which he tried to explain from within his personal experience under the tutelage of a Yaqui sorcerer known as Don Juan. Don Juan said to Carlos, "You dwell too much upon yourself . . . Seek and see the marvels all around you. You will get tired of looking at yourself alone, and that fatigue will make you deaf and blind to everything else." (from *The Teachings of Don Juan: A Yaqui Way of Knowledge* by Carlos Castaneda, University of California Press, 1968, p. 50.) Don Juan advised Carlos to seek an ally, a power that would help him, advise him, and give him the strength he needed to enhance his life, guide his acts, and further his knowledge.

Part of Don Juan's advice to Castaneda was that he should learn to see like a crow. He said, "I learned to become a crow because those birds are the most effective of all. No other birds bother them, except perhaps larger hungry eagles, but crows fly in groups and can defend themselves. Men don't bother crows either, and that is an important point. Any man can distinguish a large eagle, especially an unusual eagle, or any other large unusual bird, but who cares about a crow? A crow is safe. It is ideal in size and nature. It can go safely into any place without attracting attention." (ibid., 175)

After smoking a mixture of peyote, Castaneda felt at one point he actually turned into a crow and had the experience of having wings and flying. When it was over, Don Juan told him, "It does not take much to become a crow. You did it, and now you will always be one." He also told him that the black feathers of a crow are really silvery, and that a bird that looks dark to us looks white to a crow.

The conclusion I draw from Castaneda's hallucinogenic experience, as he described it, was that it did indeed induce a state resembling a nonordinary reality with some flashes of disassociation. He said, "I saw the world in a way that was structurally different from ordinary vision." But do we need to ingest mind-altering substances in order to have extraordinary vision? I think not. Do we need a teacher, a guru, a shaman to help us apprehend this vision in our lives? They can become bridges by which we cross from the outer world of material perceptions into the inner world of spiritual reality, but ultimately we are responsible for our own growth. We should never, never hand our lives over to anyone to try to do for us what we must do for ourselves. Many wise and wonderful teachers have appeared in my life, and I am indebted to them forever for what I have learned and for what I have become because of them. I trust new teachers are yet to come. We need each other in this world in our quest for authenticity and enlightenment, and there are great and wise souls in our midst who are here to help us. But I think it is a mistake to ever place ourselves under the dominion of anyone to the extent that we sacrifice our own particular powers or deny our own unique gifts.

In suggesting that there is something we can learn from crows, I am really talking about strengthening the connection with the luminous web of existence which holds all of us together, a topic I will discuss in more detail in the final chapter. Everything teaches us in one way or another. Every person, every creature, and every event will instruct us, if we allow it.

I had the extraordinary and humbling experience in the summer of 1998 of being initiated into a naming ceremony in the Native American tradition when I was given the name of Crow Man. It came about through a series of seemingly unrelated experiences, which I have now come to see as part of the one Great Experience of Life that binds all of us, human and nonhuman, in an indissoluble relationship with all that is now, has been, or ever will be.

There are numerous rituals in Native American culture, each varying in form and meaning, depending on tribal traditions. One such ritual is the sweat lodge, a purification ceremony comparable to baptism. Another is the ceremony of the pipe, used to express thanksgiving and gain harmony and introspection. Still another is the calling of the spirits in order to receive guidance. The Sun Dance is a death and resurrection ceremony that takes various forms but is really a prayer dance. The naming ceremony is a ritual that shows the evidence of a new power and direction in the life of the person receiving the name. It is sometimes given at the conclusion of a vision quest. The initiate may reveal what guidance or manifestation came during the vision quest, and from this will emerge a new name, a symbol of where he or she has been and where he or she is going.

After my spring morning walk, when I heard a crow call my name and began to interact with that crow and his family, I slowly began to weave bits and pieces of the experience into my sermons and the articles I wrote for the church newsletter. Some of these will appear in the following chapter, when I actually tried to give voice to Charlie the Crow. Some people experienced a resonance with what I wrote and said, some were entertained by it and thought it was cute, and others frankly thought it was drivel. I overheard one woman say to another, "When he gets on that crow kick, I just turn him off." I understand all those reactions. We all respond in different ways to what we hear. Even when it is offered out of someone's experience, if it does not resonate with our own framework of experience, we may be forced to regard it as useless.

But there was one man, listening to my sermons on the radio and reading my messages in the newsletter, who was responding with deep empathy. His name was Roy Wilson, a retired Methodist pastor and the traditional spiritual leader of the Cowlitz Indian Nation. Roy was born on the Yakima Indian Reservation of an Indian father and non-Indian mother. He grew up and was educated in two different worlds and dedicated his life to blending Native American and Christian spiritualities, to the end that both cultures might experience partnership and liberation. He has served as a Methodist pastor, tribal chairman of the Cowlitz tribe, director of the Small Tribes Organization of Western Washington, college professor and board member of St. Paul's School of Theology, and has published several books and articles on the subject of Native American Theology. Roy became my friend. I invited him to teach and participate in worship in my church, and he welcomed me to an outdoor worship service that he conducted, attended largely by Native Americans. I also invited him to share in the leadership of a five-day Spiritual Life Retreat for families from my church, which was held annually at a camp on the western shores of Puget Sound. It was at one of those retreats that Roy voluntarily conducted the naming ceremony that bestowed on me the official name of Crow Man.

The ceremony began with drumming, chanting, and smoking the pipe. When he called me to sit in the center of the circle of participants, he explained the significance of the ritual and the reason for choosing the name. It was an acknowledgment of my reverence and connection to the crow as one of the totem animals in my life. Roy's book, *A Native American Liberation Theology,* explains the power and sacred nature of this ritual. "Each tribe may have its own way of conducting the name giving ceremonies, but there are many similarities. The names are not given indiscriminately, but very purposefully. These names tell us who we are as well as informing us regarding the path we will follow in life." (p. 118)

In biblical tradition, names were considered sacred and usually represented something of the person's character or witness. Jacob, for example, had his name changed to Israel following his mystical wrestling with an angel of God, meaning that his nature had expanded and found its true spiritual calling. Saul's name was changed to Paul after his conversation to Christ. So in Native American tradition, names are considered sacred, especially those that are given in a naming ceremony for they represent a vision of a deeper truth in the person's life.

A remarkable thing happened to me as I was sitting in that circle that night. Roy was drumming and chanting. I had my eyes shut. Slowly I began to drift out of my body. I knew I was leaving, and I did not care. I was no longer in the room. I seemed to be soaring across a huge black chasm of sky to a fire circle between steep canyon walls. The drumming and chanting I had been listening to earlier became not just the voice of one but the voices of many people dancing around that fire. I remember at one point the vivid brilliance of the stars overhead that arched across the mountains, forming the canyon. I could smell the smoke, and I could see forms of people dancing in a circle, bodies burnished in the fire glow. Time seemed suspended. I was standing at the fire and receiving a new name, but I was in a place where I was completely at home and close to people that I knew loved me. When the drumming finally stopped and Roy stepped forward and touched my shoulders for the bestowing of the name, I came back into the room in the lodge and became fully present again.

It is difficult to write about those experiences that transcend the limits of our accustomed realities. Something is lost in framing them in words. All I can say is that I felt a power in my life that night which came to help me, advise me, and give me the strength to perform the acts I was given to do. The experience of leaving my body, rather than being frightening, was like a joyous reunion with a person I used to be and still am, with people I used to know and still do. It became an indispensable aid to my knowing something of the marvelous secret that the Yaqui shaman promised to Carlos Castaneda. And what is that secret? That is for each of us to discover individually, but for me that night, was a repeating of what I have always intuitively believed: *Everything is one. We are all parts of one another. There is no separation. Unity and oneness of life are the ultimate realities. There is no greater truth than this.*

I said I've always known it, but I knew it that night with a surety and clarity that were undeniable. And I knew if we could just get hold of this truth, we would stop hurting each other and fighting each other, for we would truly apprehend what Jesus Christ taught as the central ethic of spiritual living: *that which we do to others, we do to ourselves.*

When I came home from that camp with my new name of Crow Man, my driveway once again was sprinkled with a few crow feathers. I looked up at my "dark apostles," sitting quietly in the trees, acting as though I had not been away, and I said, "I am now Crow Man." Did they know? Of course they did. Not in the way you and I know things, where we depend on words being spoken or written, but in that deep inner knowing that is a vital current flowing in every living thing.

Don Juan told Castaneda, "It takes a very long time to be a proper crow." Castaneda also learned that becoming a person of knowledge was not a permanent accomplishment, but a process, and that the link between ordinary and nonordinary reality is always conditioned by our awareness. We will learn only as much as we are capable of learning at any particular time. When we are ready for more, we will learn more, until eventually the barrier that separates us from what the Yaquii called "the reality of special consensus" will be removed. Then we will know our oneness and begin to live from a new and hallowed perception.

Apostle of Darkness

All was just as it had been before—
The same downward slant to the driveway,
The lavender impatiens clustered beside the house,
The firs rising in protective solitude.
The huge black bird perched in the maple
Regarded me with a kind of stoic endurance.
I swear he yawned as I looked up.

Then suddenly something changed.
In an instant heaven descended
Like a feather in flight,
Fell on me with a blaze of glory
And in bliss too great to tell,
Filled me with a safety and freedom,
By speaking a single word: home.

Apostle of darkness I sometimes call him,
This black guardian sitting beside my door.
He said to me, "You do not need to go away.
You do not even need to listen for a voice.
The world will offer itself to you,
It will throb in ecstasy at your feet,
And everything vanished comes back as song."

I wanted the moment to linger,
But Crow had other things to do
Which had to be done before night fell.
He left me, promising he would return
And help me complete the song.
As he arced above, I saw for the first time
A silvery glint in his black cape.

Rodney R. Romney

Chapter Eight

Charlie's Chance to Speak:
A Fantasy (in case you wonder)

This chapter contains some teachings by Charlie Crow. He told them to me, and I wrote them down since Charlie does not write as we do. These teachings appear in the form of conversation we had together. Usually these conversations were dominated by Charlie. You may discover that there are very few subjects that concern us humans that Charlie does not have an opinion about.

On Stewardship

Charlie had this conversation with me while he was perched on my mailbox. I made the mistake of asking him not to sit on *my* mailbox and decorate it with his usual calling card.

"Nothing is mine or yours," said Charlie. "It is *ours*, but it's all on loan. That means it's not even ours. We just get to use it. Crows long ago mastered the art of using things without getting attached to them or trying to own them."

"Like you use the top of my mailbox as your bathroom," I suggested.

"Exactly!" chirped Charlie. "It's my mailbox as much as yours. Perhaps I should have been a bit more discreet where I made my deposit. But you humans are so finicky about those matters that it gives me a certain amount of pleasure to break your rules."

"Get on with the lecture and save the illustrations," I snapped peevishly.

"Right. Well, as I have observed, you humans spend your entire lives scrambling to make something you call 'money.' You invented this nonsense a long time ago, and I'm sure you're not going to give it up. But the problem is that you are so attached to making money and stacking it up that you have forgot the joy of just living. See that squirrel over there. He gathers nuts for the winter so he won't starve. But you gather more nuts than you could possibly eat in a lifetime. And when it comes to sharing those nuts—well, forget that. Humans watch other humans go hungry and starve, and it never occurs to them they could prevent it."

"Come on, Charlie," I protested. "You're being a bit harsh. We do help each other."

"But not enough," countered Charlie. "We would never let a crow starve who couldn't find food for itself, unless its time had come to leave. We would never let our young ones get caught in a predicament without trying to help them. Remember when that young crow fell into the stairwell at your church and couldn't get out?"

"Yes, and we helped him out and took him to a wildlife vet for wing repair. So there!"

"Yes, you did, and we are grateful. We crows cannot do everything as cleverly as you humans can. But before you came to the rescue of that youngster, all the members of the colony had gathered around and were trying to help."

"So you are saying we don't help each other?"

"I am saying you do some wonderful things, but you need to do more. You need to realize you were put here by the Great Constructor for just one reason: to help each other. You need to let go of some of the nuts you have stored. You need to turn loose of some of that precious money you have hoarded. The Great Constructor asks us to give back the things we love most. Since most of you love money the most, money is what you must give back. And by the way, you haven't left any bread out on the lawn for three days. See if I give you any more feathers.

"One final thing. When you stand in front of your congregation and try to get money out of them, just say that Charlie Crow said to tell them, 'Only you can give your money. No one else can do it for you. And only you can give your love to this world. No one else can do that for you either.' That's what stewardship is about."

With that, Charlie Crow flew off, and I was left to scrub off *our* mailbox.

On Helping Each Other

A few days later, I told Charlie a story a woman in my church had told me. This woman walks around Green Lake every day. On several occasions, she has noticed two small crows caring for and feeding a crow that was obviously older, blind, and somewhat disabled. The small ones would take turns bringing food bits and inserting them into the beak of the blind crow. I asked Charlie if such behavior is normal.

"It happens occasionally," said Charlie, "but not as frequently as older crows feeding younger ones. This was probably a pair of chicks feeding a parent who may have been injured. Most crows do not live long when they are disabled. The chances are that the blind crow will not survive. You must remember that crows are as individualistic as humans. Some are generous, compassionate, and solicitous of others, while some are selfish and inclined only toward caring for themselves. I believe we have observed that pattern in humans. Maybe that's where crows learned it. By the way, crows are the only species who share their food, who actually invite strangers to join in. Do you humans do that?"

Charlie always has to have the last word.

Gift Giving

I wasn't about to give up on the topic of giving, so one morning, I asked Charlie, "Why do you call the other crows when you see me coming with food? You could have more for yourself if you didn't alert the whole blasted neighborhood." Charlie, at the time, was in the process of attacking a piece of stale bread with his beak, while others were stocking up on softer pieces.

"We share what we have," Charlie reminded me, a theme he strikes often. "Food is the major concern for all wildlife. We work hard to survive. Not to share with others violates our own inner code."

"I've heard some barbaric stories about crows as killers. Someone told me about seeing crows attack a squirrel that was crossing a power line. They knocked the squirrel to the street and immediately set upon him and devoured him. That sounds pretty horrible."

"You don't know all the details," replied Charlie. "But your species is no different. You cage up creatures, pump them full of chemicals and feed them until they are obese, and then slaughter and eat them. Next time you sink your teeth into a lamb chop, remember that what you are doing is no different than what we are occasionally forced to do. Hunger makes fiends out of all of us. Besides, how do you know that we crows did not learn cannibalism from humans? We imitate you in many ways, unfortunately."

"Do you give gifts to one another as we do?" I asked.

"All the time," he replied. "We have some rules on gift giving. Don't give something you don't want. Give what is truly needed. Don't overgive. Humans violate all those rules. You make spoiled gluttons out of your young when you load them down with excesses. Above all, you need to learn to give yourself. Kindness, concern, and love are now and will always be the best gifts anyone can give. Let every gift you make symbolize your love; otherwise, it is a waste of your money, time, and effort."

He fluttered his wings, preparatory for takeoff, then added, "As I told you, crows are as individualistic as humans. Some are more polite and respectful than others. We are not all ruffians and bandits, as some of you believe. We have been accused of overpopulating and crowding out smaller birds. Look at yourselves. Humans are the worst overpopulators on earth. You chortle over the birth of seven babies from one mother, piously declaring that God did it." (The story had been in the paper that morning. Had Charlie read it?) "The truth is the woman took a fertility drug. You are slowly robbing the land of places for yourselves as well as wildlife. Take a good look at yourselves before it is too late. Perhaps when you humans stop overpopulating, other species will fall back into the balance that the Great Constructor designed. And remember, no crow would let another crow starve, as humans often do. Now go back to your people and tell them that Charlie Crow said, 'Give the gift that lasts, the gift of a future for you, your children, and all the species that share this earth with you.' Do that, and you will live."

With that, he flew to the top of a high tree where he sat and eyed me steadily. Finally I went inside just to escape his piercing gaze.

A Crow Convention

I was invited by Charlie Crow to sit in on a crow convention that was being held in the Richmond Beach area where I lived. "Two-legged creatures are seldom invited to these gatherings," he told me, "but we have been observing you for several years and feel you are ready. Besides, we crows like to show off, and to do that requires an audience. But you will have to sit and be quiet; otherwise, you will be asked to leave." He told me where it was to be held and what time I should show up.

I positioned myself a short distance from the grove where the convention was to be held. I could imagine how dangerous it might be to sit under the trees. Crows defecate freely, and I did not care to be one of their targets.

The crows began to arrive at first light. Their noise was unbelievable. I decided that one of the reasons crows get together is to see who can caw the longest and loudest. After a plenary session, where everyone spoke at once, sharing stories of recent harrowing experiences as well as more pleasant adventures, the delegation broke up into four workshops. These were (1) *language*, in which phrases like "eating crow" and "crowing" as synonyms for boasting were discussed and banned; there was also unanimous objection to using the term "crow's feet" as indicative of the aging process, and there was universal disapproval of the human term, *A Murder of Crows*, in referring to a colony; (2) *diet*, where good feeding areas were cited and certain restrictions placed against the old motto of crows eating anything that doesn't eat them first; (3) *fraternization*, in which crows were cautioned to avoid intimate mingling with birds who are not crows (referred to as "interspecies dating") and being extremely cautious about associations with humans (a debate that caused many eyes to turn on me); and (4) *enemies*, namely humans and their domesticated pets; strategies were offered as how to make life miserable for both.

The convention lasted the better part of a day, with a break for lunch when crows raided garbage cans in the neighborhood and came back to report on what they found. Charlie was elected Chief Crow for the coming year. He then extended an invitation to the delegation to hold their next meeting on the roof of my house. There was heated discussion over this since the roof did not offer the protection that trees afforded. The invitation was subsequently denied because "they had never done it that way before." I felt as though I were sitting through a church business meeting.

As a final gesture of goodwill, the crows voted to make me an honorary member of the Richmond Beach Colony, although it was not unanimous. The stipulations were that I must leave the lid off my garbage can and remove any others I see, run off any humans who approach the area carrying air rifles or weapons of any kind, and teach humans that crows lived here before they did and should be treated with greater respect. Also, I am to tell the members of my clan that we have much to learn about other species who share this planet with them and that we need to stop thinking of ourselves as superior. As Charlie Crow reminded me, "I can fly to your church faster than you can get there in your car, and it costs me nothing."

Charlie told the gathering that they planned to teach me *crow-ese*, and if I do well at it, he will then begin giving me flying lessons. There was an uproar of laughter over that.

The convention closed with the reading of this verse (for my benefit, I believe):

Consider the crows that live in your trees, they toil not and neither do they spin, yet Solomon in all his glory was not arrayed like one of these.

I was personally grateful that they voted against having next year's convention on my roof. I was not eager to clean up the mess they would leave behind, and besides, what would the neighbors think? Charlie thinks I am too fastidious and overly concerned about such unimportant matters.

Tolerance

The most important lesson I learned from Charlie was on tolerance. "Tolerance," he said to me one day, as though he had been thinking about it for some time but was waiting for the right moment, "is not simply putting up with something. Tolerance is allowing everything the right to be. This means without your interference, without your directives, without your judgments."

"But there are evils and injustices in this world," I protested. "Are we supposed to tolerate those, pretend that they don't matter, and just allow them to be?"

Charlie shrugged one wing. "You do not have the power to change anything outside yourself. That which you condemn will in turn condemn you. That which you judge harshly, you will someday become. The only thing you can do effectively is to love. But before you can love, you must learn to bless. And before you can bless, you must learn to tolerate. That means the only true change you can effect in this world is in yourself and your own inner experience."

He saw the confusion registering itself on my face. But before I could open my mouth to mount an argument, he went on. "Unconditional love is what we all receive from God. If your parents did their job, then you learned it from them. If they didn't, you can learn it from others. That is what your wonderful churches are supposed to be doing, but too many of them are built on the belief that there is something terribly wrong in creation that needs to be fixed."

"And you don't think there is?" I asked.

"No. The fault is not in creation. The fault is in belief systems that view certain persons and certain species as wrong and expendable. The only thing wrong in creation is a lack of love, particularly among you humans. Churches are supposed to bless relationships, teach people to love each other and honor all creation, help everyone affirm and enjoy life with everyone and everything who share it on this planet. Instead, many of your churches are busy putting labels on people, labels that define who's in and who's out, who's good and who's bad. When you do this, you are not tolerating life. You are killing it."

"I think I've got it, Charlie. It's just hard for me to get away from making comparisons. But all things are not good. Some things are bad."

"There's a reason for that," replied Charlie. "You would never really know what good is if you did not know its opposite. You would never know love had you not experienced hate. But once you see the destructiveness of these negative attitudes and actions, you will stop making your judgments, which in the end only become judgments against yourself."

He looked at me closely and then cawed softly, "This is a lot for you to embrace all at once. Just work on it for a while. And remember this, everything, absolutely everything, is here for a purpose. There is never a justifiable reason for killing, as you do to your offenders, as you do to the insects and rodents that get in your way. Know that every species that is here makes it possible for you to live. Even the tiniest insect is contributing to your stay on this planet."

"But animals eat each other. They even eat insects," I demurred, not wanting to concede the argument.

"Life supports life," he answered. "When you are wiser, you will understand that rule. But killing just to get rid of something, or because you get a thrill out of taking life, are grievous offenses, and you will pay dearly for such actions. Indeed, you are already paying, as your children begin to take up guns and kill. Well, I can see you have heard enough for one day. There is more for you to learn when you are ready. I have come to be your ally and to help you find your way to a higher truth. When you need me, I will be there. You can depend on it."

He flew off, tucking his feet under his body as he mounted into the sky. He left me earthbound but not abandoned, listening to the feelings in my heart, the questions in my mind, all overridden by the sure knowing in my soul that I was not and never would be alone. I had a spiritual ally who assured me that the One who had created me in Truth, Light, and Love had a grand purpose for me and all creation. If tolerance could lead me in the direction of that purpose, I had everything to gain and nothing to lose. Nothing except my chains. Nothing except my judgments. Nothing except my anguish. Nothing except my confusion. Tolerance, as Charlie Crow said, is allowing *everything* the right to be what it is—even me.

The White Crow Theory

I asked Charlie if he had ever seen a white crow. At first he was reluctant to talk about it and wanted to know where I had heard about such a thing. So I related the following information to him. A famous author and scholar by the name of Dr. William James, in his 1896 presidential address to the

Society for Psychical Research, talked about the "White Crow Metaphor" by saying, "If you wish to upset the law that all crows are black, you must not seek to show that all crows are black; it is enough to prove one single crow can be white." He told the story of a trance medium named Mrs. Piper, who led him beyond all acceptable and common beliefs that were held by the scientific world of his day. His theory was that the world isn't what it appears to be on the surface and that there are bigger realities than just physical appearances. He predicted that the day would come when scientists and mystics alike would acknowledge that previous theories are not enough to explain life's present-day realities and that the universe is a connected Whole that supports all forms of life in loving, benevolent ways.

When I finished, I asked Charlie Crow, "Are there such creatures as white crows?"

Charlie answered, "You will see a white crow when you are ready to be changed by what it might teach you and not until. Just remember there are always variables to any theory you might wish to propound." As he finished speaking, Charlie stared off into the distance.

Then I saw it—a tiny, little white spot on his breast. I stared at it more closely. Was it a scar, a wound, a single white feather, like a single strand of gray hair? "You have—" I began, "that is, you must be—" I stopped. The white spot seemed to extend itself for a moment to his entire wing. I could only gasp, "You have a white wing."

"And you are *the victim of a white wing conspiracy*," laughed Charlie. With that, he flew away, leaving me wordless and mouth agape.

There are albinos in every species. Native Americans used to believe a white buffalo was a symbol of supernatural power. Could there really be a white crow? Or does this theory mean that when we grow to a new understanding of life that goes beyond the ordinary into the realm of the mystical, or to a nonordinary reality, as Castaneda described it, we reach a mystery that transcends our normal states of knowing. At that level, the "white crow theory" becomes not a theory but a door that leads beyond common belief into a new realm of thinking and acting.

Once I saw Jesus Christ purely and simply as the Lord and Savior of my life. Today I realize it doesn't matter if the Christ who fills our vision is that historical Jesus, the Cosmic Ruler of the Universe, or the divine presence in my neighbor. These are only aspects of his being. In whatever aspect he is most real to us, what matters is that we love him and seek to follow him. In a sense, Jesus transcends our knowing because he himself was a white crow. Rather than asking us to subscribe to a pietistic obedience to rules and doctrines, he said it is enough that we love God and our neighbors as we love ourselves. He knew that loving transcends all levels of knowing.

> When you can go no further
> And think you have reached the limits,
> It is time to go back,
> To reassess where you have been
> And to save what can be saved.
> Let mystery have its place in you,
> And if a bird sings in the branches
> Do not rush forward to tame it.
> If something new lights in your heart,
> Let it take shape and grow.
> The time will eventually come
> When the mystery will be solved
> When what is not known now
> Will become crystal clear,
> And you will take a step closer
> To the truth we all seek.

Rodney R. Romney

Chapter Nine

A Crow's Version of the Creation Story

The opening pages of the Hebrew Bible offer a creation story which has profoundly influenced religious thinking for thousands of years. This story was not intended to be a scientific treatise on how the world came into being, but it is obviously an inspired writing, or it would not have survived. Other religious traditions have their individual stories of the earth's origin. To the Celts, the crow was associated with creation of the world, while to the Athapaskan Indians of Alaska, Crow was the Creator. In Northwest Native American mythology, animals are cultural heroes, representing both evil and good. Crow (or Raven) is one of the most frequently used characters in these ancient stories, probably because of its intelligence. It is found in ancient stories as well as on carvings on totem poles today, including a pole in my own yard. This pole was carved from a cedar tree by a wood-carver of the Haidi tribe and presented to me as a gift from a friend. When asked by Fred the carver what three animals I wanted on the totem, without hesitation I replied, "Wolf, whale, and crow."

He squinted at me speculatively. "You have chosen well, one from each group—the furred, the finned, and the feathered."

When the totem was completed and erected in my yard, Fred came with his family to do a ceremonial dance that would breathe spirit into the totem animals. This beautifully carved pole is my daily visual reminder of a mythology that has enhanced human wisdom throughout generations and the spiritual strength these traditions still inspire today.

Shortly after the pole was completed, I composed the following fable. It is purely a product of my own spiritual imagination in which Crow is featured not as Creator but as one assigned with Wolf and Whale to the lesser but vital role of Cocreators. As such, their work was to help the other creatures, including humans, understand their place in the great scheme of creation.

Prologue

In the beginning was the Universe.
Billions of galaxies and solar systems
whirled and exploded for billions of years.
In one of those solar systems was born
a tiny speck of dust to be named Earth.
Earth was a fireball for a million years
as it spun and twirled in the galaxies.
Then, when the fire had burned out,
rocks, oceans, continents, and mountains
slowly began to emerge and take shape,
followed by trees, flowers of scented color,
and creatures who moved by their own power.
Some of the creatures crawled on the earth,
some swam in the oceans and rivers,
and some soared through the skies.
Then came a creature named Human who
walked on two legs, talked with One called God,
and gave names to all the other creatures.
And the earth and all its creatures waited
to see if Human was a blessing or a curse.

The Fifth Day of Creation

And God said, "Let the waters bring forth swarms of living creatures, and let birds fly above the earth across the firmament of the heavens." So God created the great sea monsters and every living creature that moves, with which the waters swarm, according to their kinds, and every winged bird, according to its kind. And God saw that it was good.

—Genesis 1:20-23, Revised Standard Version

Crow flew cawing to the top of a tall tree overlooking the ocean. At the same moment, Whale surfaced from the water, spouting water from his blowhole. Crow watched silently for a moment then threw back his head and cried, "Caw." Whale looked up at Crow and sent forth a shrill but plaintive whine.

"Do you know where we are?" asked Crow.

"I don't even know who we are," replied Whale. "This is all new to me."

"Me too," said Crow. "I don't remember being here before. Of course, I don't remember being anywhere before."

"No one's been here before," croaked Whale in liquid tones, "because this is only the fifth day of creation." With that, the whale dropped back into the ocean, flipping his tail skyward and creating a splash that spread across the watery surface.

"Ugly creature," noted Crow, to no one in particular. "I notice it has no feathers. I think I'll dive down in the water and take a closer look."

"You can't do that," came a voice from the shoreline. "You're not made to swim."

Crow looked down and saw a white bird floating on the water. It was a seagull. "But you have feathers, and you're swimming. Obviously there have been some mistakes in this process called creation."

"I think not," protested the seagull. "I do remember a voice speaking at the first moment I arrived here, and it said, 'That's good, if I say so myself.'"

"I heard that voice, too," said Crow. "But that huge slimy creature out there in the water. Ugh! Clearly a mistake."

"Not so!" gurgled a salmon as it stuck its head from beneath the surface of the ocean where it had been listening. "I was told I was good too. We are all good, even though we are all different."

Crow pondered this a long time for he knew that this was the truth and that he must not forget it. From that moment on, Crow resolved to judge less and listen more.

Just then Whale resurfaced on the water. "Come on down," he called to Crow. "We need to talk. Just land on my back. I'll give you a ride you won't forget."

Crow hesitated a moment, then spread his wings, and flew from the tree, over the water's edge, and lit on the sleek, shiny back of Whale. He skidded a little on his landing but managed to stay upright. "You're slippery," he said to Whale.

"Hang on," Whale answered. "I'll float while we talk. I also heard the voice saying that I was good. It was the first thing I heard. We are all good. But there is more to come. There will soon be other creatures running about on the land. They may be dangerous."

Crow pondered a moment. "If the voice said we are good, then whoever or whatever comes must also be good. We can only wait and see what happens. Apparently some of us are made to swim in water, and some of us are made to fly in the sky. Who comes next may not be as well equipped as we are. We must be ready to help them." He dug his feet into Whale's shiny back as he reflected on what that might mean.

"Oooh, that tickles," said Whale. "You have very sharp little feet."

"And you have none," said Crow. "Why is that?"

"I have fins," said Whale. "They help me swim. Water is where I live. You have wings. They help you fly. Sky is where you live. We have been given exactly what we need. Come back tomorrow. We will need to talk more. There is a creature coming who is supposed to give names to all of us. But I think we have already found our own names."

Crow reached down with his beak and gave a playful little jab to Whale's shiny back. Then he spread his wings and flew back to his tree. As he did, he saw another crow gazing at him with shy and brilliant eyes. He had a glad sense of knowing that he had just found another part of himself.

The Sixth Day

And God said, "Let the earth bring forth living creatures, according to their kinds: cattle and creeping things and beasts of the earth according to their kinds." And it was so . . . And God saw that it was good.

—Genesis 1:24-25

Wolf paused at the edge of the forest. He lifted his head, sniffing deeply of the cool air with its many-wafted scents, and he threw back his head and howled. As his cry soared into the air, it startled Crow who was just waking up from his nest with his newfound mate. Looking down, Crow saw Wolf standing lone and uncertain, a green fire glistening in his eyes as he gazed curiously at the world before him.

"Welcome," said Crow. "Whale, who lives in the water, said you would be arriving. I am Crow who flies in the sky. Who are you?"

"I do not know who I am," came back the growling answer. "I don't even know where I am."

"You are on earth, and this is the sixth day of creation. I will call you Wolf because your cry sounds like a woof. I am Crow because my cry sounds like a caw. Whale makes a sound that sounds like a high-pitched gentle wail, so he is called Whale."

"Are we allowed to name ourselves?" asked Wolf.

"Yes, although we think there is a creature coming who may decide to rename us. We are expecting that one to arrive any time now. Meanwhile, welcome to this wonderful earth. Come down to the shore, and I will introduce you to Whale."

Wolf followed Crow, who flew above him and led him to the edge of the shore where the waves lapped gently on the sand. Whale was waiting out in the deeper water. "Come on out," he called.

"Oh dear," said Crow. "Wolf has neither wings nor fins. He only has, well, let's see, he only has fur and feet."

"But I have sharp teeth," protested Wolf, opening his mouth to prove it.

From his position offshore, Whale roared with pleasure and sent a spout of water into the air. "We all bring something different," he cried. "And we have all been told we are good."

"I heard something else," said Wolf. "I heard there is a strange creature coming called Human, that it will be ugly, awkward, and unbelievably helpless. But it will also be dangerous."

"Then Human must be the error," declared Crow, determined that there must be something wrong somewhere in this whole scheme of creation.

"Human will be the puzzle," replied Whale. "Human will either be our friend or our enemy. We must wait and see. I have thought about this a long time. I believe Human will be physically inept but will have a cunning and sharp mind, capable of great good as well as great harm. It will need our help to understand its place in the world."

"Is there any way to prevent his coming?" shuddered Wolf. "Could we present a petition to the Voice who created us, suggesting it not make Human?"

"Too late," intoned Crow. "Human is already on the drawing board. May even be here now. And I do not think the Voice is going to be greatly influenced by what we say."

"But if the Voice has called everything good so far, then Human will also be good," declared Whale. "Perhaps that will be our task. To help that goodness come forth."

The three talked together awhile and then decided to retreat and wait for tomorrow to come. Whale sank to the ocean floor and lay brooding beneath the waves. Wolf went back into the forest and sank down in some tall grass, grimly pondering the future. Crow flew back to the top of the tree, shivering a bit in uncertainty. They all felt their wonderful new world was going to be changed, and those changes both frightened and intrigued them.

As night fell, all creation groaned together in apprehension, waiting for the appearance of Human.

The Seventh Day

Then God said, "Let us make humans in our image, after our likeness, and let them have dominion over the fish of the sea, and over the birds of the air, and over every thing that creeps upon the earth." So God created humans in the image of God: male and female God created them. And God blessed them, and gave them dominion over the fish of the sea and over the birds of the air and over every living thing that moves upon the earth . . . And God saw everything that had been made, and behold, it was very good. And there was evening and morning, a sixth day.

—Genesis 1:26-31, free translation

They met together at the shore on the morning of the seventh day—the crow, the whale, and the wolf.

"Well, this is a fine kettle of fish!" grumbled the Whale, usually the optimist. "A few days ago, we were pretty much alone here, Crow and I. Then came Wolf, a four-legged creature, who looked as though he might devour us at any moment. And now, just an hour ago, I saw the strangest creature of all. Two Humans came down here to the water and lowered themselves in it to bathe. They squealed and jumped around a bit and then got out. Strangest sight I've ever seen."

"I saw them," said Crow disgustedly. "Humans are grotesque. They have neither feathers nor fins, neither wings nor claws. They are skinny with tiny clumps of fur here and there on their bodies. They can't fly, and they can't stay underwater more than a few minutes. Besides, they are weaklings. I don't think they can even lift themselves."

Wolf snorted. "When they saw me, I heard them say, 'I wonder if he would be good to eat?' As though they didn't have enough fruit on the trees or vegetables in the ground to keep them from going hungry. I am wondering if *they* might be good to eat. But then I have been wondering that about both of you, ever since I got here."

"Small chance of that, old man," growled Whale, "since you can't swim very far nor fly at all. If I wanted, I could certainly eat both you and this silly bird."

"Wait a minute," said Crow. "Do you see what is happening. We are starting to turn against each other. We must not quarrel. I think we have been given an enormous assignment. We have to educate the Humans. They were not given the insights that were given to us."

"But I heard the Voice say they were to have dominion over all the other creatures of the earth," protested Wolf. "What does dominion mean?"

"I have no idea," muttered Whale. "How could anything so puny have dominion over me? Why, I am the largest creature on the earth."

"Let's see," mused Crow. "*Domine* from the Latin, meaning God. It must have something to do with the Voice we all heard when we were created, the Voice that created us."

"Good grief," growled Wolf. "Is Latin what you learn up in the trees?"

"But the Voice was kind," insisted Crow, ignoring Wolf's last remark. "If it gave even a part of that kindness to Humans, then we have nothing to fear. Don't you see. That's what dominion means. It means to give a bit of God to each other. It doesn't mean to rule or destroy. It means we have each been given a part of the Voice, and that's all we have to share."

"We have only to wait and see," agreed Whale. "Look, here they come."

Man and Woman were walking together to the shore.

"She looks prettier than he," noted Wolf, "but both look slightly stupid."

The humans came to the edge of the shore. A silent hush fell over Crow, Whale, and Wolf as they waited to see what their next move should be.

The humans looked around. They saw the whale staring at them from the water. They saw the wolf waiting warily next to the edge of the forest. And they saw the crow sitting on a branch above their heads and watching them intently.

For a few tiny seconds, all creation wondered and waited, knowing that a new chapter of their story was about to be written and knowing that the outcome of that story depended how everyone, including the humans, would treat the gifts of creation that had been given to them.

> **Crow, Wolf, and Whale looked at the world, strewn with seas,**
> **Littered with mountains that fell away into the distance,**
> **They looked at the creatures assembled together,**
> **To be the engineers of this infinite engine,**
> **And they felt utterly helpless.**
> **"How can we do it?" they wondered.**
> **But the word was inside them and would not be silenced.**
> **"God saw everything that had been made,**
> **And behold it was very good."**
> **The hope, the torment of hope, the patience of hope—**
> **All were buried in that word,**
> **And only in knowledge of that word could they live**
> **And create the love that must be their companion.**

Rodney R. Romney

Chapter Ten

The Luminous Web of Creation

Those of us who write—whether history, philosophy, poetry, or fiction—must finally face up to the fact that we are not creating when we write; we are simply recording what life has given to us. The best writing gathers up the fabric of one's life story and weaves it, consciously or not, into the words that get sprinkled onto a page. We are, each and every one of us, the product of our own life journey, and nothing can ever completely circumvent or allow us to disregard that truth. Writing is one way we recapture our stories. It is a way for us to remember who we came here to be and what we came here to do.

That has been as true for Soern Kierkegaard, Dietrich Bonhoeffer, Paul Tillich, Evelyn Underhill, Thomas Merton, John Steinbeck, Barbara Kingsolver, and Ivan Doig (a few of the many writers who have influenced, inspired, or intrigued me) as it is true for Rod Romney. My literary achievements do not begin to equal theirs, but our source is the same. The truest source for any writer is and will always be the self of the writer. We are our stories. We report what we know, based on what has happened to us. It is at the level of our True Self that we touch God.

So this little piece of writing is not really about a crow. It is about me. It began about as far back as memory will take me to an obscure mountain canyon in the Little Lost River Valley in Idaho, where I spent several early-boyhood summers with my father and older brothers, Dan and Dick. It was there I became acquainted with the Gray Jay, which is part of the Corvidae family. Less flashy than its cousins—the Steller's Jay, magpie, and crow—in fact downright drab in comparison, the Gray Jay is known by the rather unflattering nickname of Camp Robber because of its tendency to collect around campsites or backyards of homes in search of food bits he might filch. My father taught us to call them Camp Robbers and condemned them as pests.

My dad, the most enigmatic and yet one of the most singularly important persons in my life story, is now and forever a mystery only partially solvable.

He left his home in Murray, Utah, when he was old enough to take charge of his life and migrated north to the Little Lost River Valley. There he would spend the rest of his life in a futile search for gold. Heaving himself against those closed-away hills in search of a lode that never chose to be found, he eventually grew as solitary and unreachable as the mountain domain he had chosen. He married my mother, a daughter of one of the valley ranchers, when she was sixteen, took her into his austere canyon domain and his one-room log cabin, where she stayed long enough to produce three sons—I being the final product of their union. The canyon was not hospitable territory to my mother, nor apparently was her relationship to my father. Their marriage fully collapsed when I was three; and she left, first taking us back to the ranch in the valley, where her parents were scrubbing out a narrow living on stubborn soil and short growing seasons, and later to the little town of Arco.

It was during one of those seasonal swaps, which my estranged parents must have somehow managed to arrange for their progeny, that I became entranced with the bold and perky little birds that haunted my father's cabin. Perhaps it was boredom, lack of friends, and numbing inactivity. Whatever it was, I became intrigued with their saucy manner, their loud throaty calls that sounded like *jree, jree, jree,* and their proclivity toward socialization with a wide-eyed, towheaded little boy, who had begun to study and observe their every move. I started saving pieces of bread in my pockets at meals, and when no one was looking, I sneakily carried them out to the noisy little bandits who sat waiting in the trees above the clearing next to the cabin. I knew that my father would frown on such wasteful use of the precious and hard-earned provisions he had transported from the little hamlet of Arco more than sixty miles away. So I was careful not to bring my misguided benevolence under the scrutiny of this man who, though soft spoken, left me with the feeling that emotions lay beneath the surface that were best left undisturbed.

The Camp Robbers responded instantly to the little kitchen thief as one of their own kind and were always ready to identify me with a maddening giveaway squawk of *check, check, check.* My father became annoyed with their incessant noise and suspected someone was feeding them. He gave us strict orders not to encourage the brash beggars in any way, and if they continued to be bothersome and impertinent, he would have to shoot them.

I was stricken with guilt and fear that my indulgence might result in their destruction, but I did not know how to stop what I had started. By now the jays knew me as their benefactor and always heralded my appearance with a fanfare of shrill cries. My father, sensing my culpability, began to insist that I come with him and my two older brothers every day to the mine. They were old enough to work with him, pushing the tramcar along a track that ran into the dark interior of the mine, whose dirt sides and roof were braced by heavy timbers. There they filled the car with excavated rock and soil and pushed it back out to dump onto a pile of slag. They did not particularly relish this hard and painful toil, but it kept them occupied and made them feel useful by giving assistance to my father.

I was too young to participate in that grueling labor, but I was no longer allowed to stay alone in the cabin and cultivate my friendship with my culprit friends. On the sage-covered slope near the mine, I passed away time by catching grasshoppers with my bare hands, putting them in an empty tobacco can, and then turning them loose after I had encouraged them to spit out "tobacco juice," a brown substance which they ejected when tickled with a weed. My childish imagination associated their brief confinement in the aromatic tobacco can with their involuntary emission of "tobacco juice." But my heart was really with the brownish bluebirds, whose nests were in the trees and cool confines of the canyon floor. Eventually, when I was no longer the supplier to stoke their habit, the Camp Robbers left and haunted other territories. But I felt something rich and fulfilling had been yanked from my life, increasing the isolation I felt within myself in that beautiful but hard-bitten place.

I have to ask myself several questions today. Have I only come full circle, returning to an interrupted childhood game and an unsatisfied longing that have been smoldering in my mind for more than half a century? Possibly there is a bit of that. But I believe it is much more. I see it as my slow but persistent wakening to a spiritual reality that has been leading me into a dynamic consciousness that beats at the heart of the universe and which takes me into what can only be described as the Luminous Web of Creation that connects, integrates, and transforms everything into a unified reality. Beyond the diversity of the cosmos, there is a living, breathing force that calls for relationship and unity. This energy has been around since the universe was born and is the essence of the force and passion we sometimes call God. All life in the universe is a manifestation of this energy, which means all life is one. As wilderness explorer John Muir puts it, "Everything is hitched to everything else." You pick up one thing, only to find it connected to everything else.

Humans were not created to live on this planet alone. But if we continue our patterns of abuse, destruction, and exploitation of nature—its creatures and resources—we will soon be looking at the end of nature and, ultimately, at our own extinction. If there is a single lesson that I have learned from the jays in the canyon and the crows in my yard it is that God is inside their feathered bodies as much as inside my skin and yours. I offer no apologies for the fact that I am therefore a pan*en*theist, in that I see God as both immanent and transcendent. God is in all things, while yet above all things. In essence, God is all there is since God indwells and inhabits every single scrap of creation.

Scientists today are alarmed by the rapid loss of plant and animal species on our planet and predict our descendants will inherit a biologically impoverished world if we do not check our exploding population growth and begin an aggressive plan to save wildlands and vanishing species. Thomas Banyacya, a Hopi elder, travels around the world to share a simple but eloquent message, "If humanity doesn't stop assaulting the Earth, the Earth will start assaulting humanity." Eminent environmentalist Bill McKibben argues that we are facing a natural disaster of unparalleled magnitude because of the damage we have done to the planet, unless we voluntarily restrain ourselves from continuing to overpopulate the earth and turn back to nature, giving it room to recover from the damage we have inflicted.

The sun is setting on many endangered species, which are being pushed off the land and poached out of existence. We have broken our relationship with the earth. We have damaged the Luminous Web of Existence, which was given to us on the day of creation. Our greatest work of justice in the new millennium will be to the earth, which cries out to us daily to restore the relationships we have damaged with it, with other humans and with all creatures who share the earth with us.

While we live at a time of unprecedented peril, we also live at the most marvelous moment in human history. We are at the beginning of a "conscious evolution," as humans become aware of the processes of creation and begin to participate consciously and deliberately in fulfilling their destined role as saviors rather than destroyers. We are on a path that can best be described as a Return to the Center, the place where there are no separating barriers between one living thing and another.

This means that Charlie Crow, I, and every other living thing are individual expressions of the inseparable oneness of all life. This is not a new idea that is just being developed. It is an ancient idea that is finally being liberated. For a brief moment of time, Charlie Crow and I have shared in a silent language, which the Divine Mind of the Universe is constantly speaking through all life. This Mind tells us there are no boundaries separating us from each other, except the boundaries we have created in the dark illusions of our minds.

J. Allen Boone expressed it well in his marvelous little book *Kinship with All Life* when he said, "Behind every object which the senses can identify, whether the object be human, animal, tree, mountain, planet, or anything else, and right where the object seems to be, is the mental and spiritual fact functioning in all its completeness and perfection." (p. 62)

What is that fact? Simply stated, it is this: all things are one in the great overall plan and purpose of life. The Great Mind of the Universe is moving through everything, everywhere in a ceaseless rhythm of harmonious kinship, sharing its immensity, power, intelligence, and boundless love for creation and all its creatures.

There are four covenantal partners established in any version of the Creation Story you might choose to read—the Creator, the earth, its creatures, and humans. Humans were given the monumental task of acting as cocreators with the Creator. The goodness, wisdom, harmony, and love of God live within all aspects of creation, and we are invited to live accordingly. Our cruel and destructive domination of nature has led us to this brink of disaster. This will not change until we have a deep and personal encounter with God and seek atonement for our cultural misuse of the planet and our widespread abuse of its creatures.

Jewish mystic Abraham Heschel wrote that man's sin is in his failure to live what he is. Until we know that we are all sons and daughters of God, we will not recover the mystical relationship with nature that leads us toward universal redemption. In the mystical language of the Apostle Paul, "All creation waits with eager longing for the revealing of the sons and daughters of God . . . when it will be set free from its bondage to decay and obtain the glorious liberty of the children of God" (Romans 8:19-21).

I am not so naive as to suggest that Nature itself is totally benign. What is good for the coyote may not be good for the fawn. Yet even in the face of life living off other forms of life, there is some inscrutable, ecstatic plan within the mystery of creation, which we humans have never fully entered into. It is a plan that calls for peace and justice, not only among the diverse peoples of the earth but among all its creatures and the earth itself. There is a luminous web that unites everything together in one grand enterprise. I return often to the mantra that I believe was given to me some years ago as the heart of my life message:

> *Everything is one. We are all parts of one another. There is no separation. Unity and oneness of life are the ultimate realities. There is no greater truth than this.*

My experiences with Charlie Crow and family have only reinforced this truth for me. This book, through purely imaginative at times, is not just a fantasy or a memoir of a piece of my life. It is a call to personal renewal, a call to restore relationship, and a call to redeem ourselves and our earth, while there is still time.

Charlie taught me that crows can be as individualistic as humans. One way I observed that individualism expressed was in the manner they approached their food. There were those who called the others to the table. This was followed by a hierarchical pattern of the oldest crows eating first, while the younger ones obediently held back and waited their turn. During the nesting season, the male crow would fill its beak with as much food as possible and fly in a direct line back to the nest, where the female was sitting on the eggs.

But I observed one crow who broke all the rules. This crow stockpiled as much food in his beak as possible, then flew to a nearby tree where it sat and watched the others eat. It did not eat the bread in its beak; it simply sat and waited. When there was no more food, the few unlucky crows, who were at the bottom of the pecking order, made futile prods at the ground where there had once been food. At that moment, the crow with food stacked in its beak would attempt to alert the others to the fact that he had food and they did not. This was difficult to do since he could not get his beak open, so his cry was only a harsh, guttural noise in the throat.

I first saw him as the consummate selfish consumer who hoards what he has, not so he can share it, but simply for the pleasure of having food when the others do not. But then I was struck by how this odd posture was in some perverse way a representation of the worst kind of religion. How often have I seen religious bodies piously declare theirs was the only truth and all other truths were inferior. Only those who could recite the proper creeds and give utterance to the right doctrines could be rescued from the exile that has befallen all humanity. Like the crow who doesn't eat the bread because more than anything else he wants others to know he has bread, religious institutions are often so busy proclaiming their superiority that their adherents never really partake of the bread of life for themselves. If they did, they would have to change. They would be called to share eloquently and passionately the good news of a God who is everywhere and in everything, loving all equally and unconditionally, and calling us to live in covenant with every living creature. This is the luminous web of creation where what is inside is also outside and where the deepest yearning in everything, from the tiniest insect to the mightiest animal, is for communion, relationship, unity, and oneness.

I was sitting out on the deck one late afternoon in early fall. I had written the final chapter of this book and was in some kind of dreamscape of my own. I could hear the gurgle of the creek at the bottom of the ravine and feel the autumn sun making a final concession to warmth as it fell on my face. I began to drift into that land between waking and sleeping, where we stroll briefly in two worlds at once.

Suddenly I heard above all other sounds the soft and lulling *qwark* that a crow makes to its mate or its children. I have heard it before in the tallest trees, often in late afternoons, when the crows' constant search for food has gone into temporary suspension, and they are expressing their affection to one another. But this time it seemed closer, near at hand. I opened my eyes. There on a branch that stretched horizontally from the trunk of a huge fir in the ravine, almost on a level with my eyes, I saw a crow. It took me a moment to realize he was looking at me and that the *qwarking* sound was being directed at me. He was saying "thank you" and "well done." In tones reserved for those closest to him, in language both abstruse and revelatory, he was speaking the word to me that everyone longs to hear. That word is love. Love replaces fear. Love eliminates despair. Love overcomes the illusion of separation. Love renews all aspects of creation. Love was the first word spoken. Love will be the last. It is fitting that this little story ends with that word of love, as it was spoken by a crow.

As I told you, Charlie always has to have the last word

There Is a Crow Inside Me

There is a crow inside my mind,
Eyes alert to the invading kind,
Feet gripping tightly on the solid branches,
Ready for flight if danger advances.
I keep the crow because sky gave it, you see,
And will not let go either crow or me.

There is a crow inside my heart,
Prankster, imp, clown, upstart.
It unties aprons and children's shoelaces,
Uses feathers to tickle old people's faces.
I keep the crow because sun gave it, you see,
And will not let go either crow or me.

There is a crow inside my spirit,
Philosopher, artist, cleric, and poet,
Warbling songs in an underbrush of dreams,
Preaching sermons to the woods and streams.
I keep the crow because wind gave it, you see,
And will not let go either crow or me.

There is a crow inside my soul,
Wild, untrammeled, wanting the whole,
Pushing against all boundaries of knowing,
Yearning to fly where free winds are blowing.
I keep the crow because God gave it, you see,
And will not let go either crow or me.

Rodney R. Romney

Postlude

In the year 2000, as I reached the age of seventy, I knew it was time for me to retire from the position of senior minister of Seattle First Baptist Church. Since we had been there twenty years, the decision brought a period of mourning. But it was clear to both Beverly and me that we needed to leave Seattle and begin that new chapter of life called retirement in a different place.

We decided to move back to Idaho, the place we had always called home since it was where I was born and the place where we had met and were married. We sold our much-loved Seattle home and purchased one in the town of Idaho Falls. On the morning we were to leave, I walked out in the yard for one final glimpse of Charlie and company. But the trees were all empty of life. Not a single bird was in their branches. It was as though they refused to be part of the human ritual of saying good-bye. We drove away without looking back.

Although our home in Idaho Falls is not far from the Snake River, we have yet to see a crow in our yard. It is well that Charlie and family did not follow us here. They would not enjoy the harsh winters of this area. I still have a warm place for them in my heart; and whenever I see a crow, I send a silent message of gratitude for that chapter in my life that was filled abundantly and joyously by Charlie Crow and family. My life was broadened and enriched on that day when I heard him call my name.

May we all live in peace and harmony with each other and with the magnificent variety of species that inhabit our earth. We are all a part of one another in a strange but tender way.

A Wing's Shadow

For Rev. Rodney Romney on his retirement as the pastor
of Seattle First Baptist Church for twenty years

Here, no fist, no trumpet bell,
But a great stillness
opens like the space Simeon knew and strode through
From Messiah to Maker.

No white dove yet, no eagle above it all,
but a steady rustle
of dark feathered souls takes this opened space
And gains height.

Fools? Birdbrains?
Holy fools? Heretics?
Who stands as sentinel? Who is it risks
So many wings

To utter heresy
to let fly
to make way for the new life
Of you and me?

Muriel Nelson
Poet and Member of Seattle First Baptist Church
June 25, 2000